THE FOLSOM PRISON DAYBOOK OF DESPAIR, GRIEF, HOPE AND ART

∽

365 Poems & Meditations

By
Convict Poets of the Inside Circle
at Folsom Prison

Edited by
Bernard Gordon

Forwards by
Don Morrison & Rob Allbee

INSIDE CIRCLE

Publisher: Profit Process Books
Book design: Stefano Landini - www.stefanolandini.com

ISBN 978-0-578-88468-4

Printed in the United States of America

First Edition

Disclaimer: *The following book (the work) is for entertainment and informational purposes only. Most of the books will be given away. Any income from the incidental sale of the book, in excess of costs, shall be used for the mission of The Inside Circle. The use of any portion of the contents of the work are at the user's sole risk. Neither the Inside Circle, the authors, nor anyone else associated with the work shall be liable for loss, injury, or damages that result through the use of information provided in the work or any work derived from it. The authors, the publisher, and any others associated with the work make no representation as to the accuracy, completeness or validity of any information or advice in the work. While reasonable caution has been taken to provide accurate information and advice, the user is solely responsible for the consequences of any decisions based on the contents of the work. Any advice given is the author's own, based on his experience. If in doubt, always seek the advice of a professional who can advise you appropriately before taking any action based on the work's contents.*

Dedication

Most people who knew him, would not consider Patrick Nolan a prince, but he was more than that. He had maneuvered through a violent childhood of domestic abuse, which escalated and led to the loss of his mother through suicide. Eventually Patrick escaped Nova Scotia to the streets of California, full of dope, despair, and broken expectations, where he hustled to stay alive.

There, Patrick killed a man, was convicted, and sentenced to life in prison without the possibility of parole (LWOP) in one of California's worst prisons while still a teenager. Assaults, stabbings, riots, and death were constants. Despite these gruesome realities, Patrick found meaning for his life and became dedicated to becoming a shrewd convict activist for healing and recovery.

Patrick got his poetry published which led to his relationship with a mentor and father-figure, in Don Morrison. Don loved poetry and became one of the co-founders of the self-help program at Folsom—The Men's Support Group.

But Patrick was the lynch pin to initiating this program with his unique understanding and acceptance of the difficulties and realities of prison. With the determination to acquire the support of correctional officers, administration, free staff, outside volunteers, and prisoners, he was instrumental in birthing a movement.

Nolan had a vision for the power of poetry and a vision about healthy masculinity. He acted on them by developing both visions to create what was needed and what he was hungry for.

He brought outside poets together to form and teach classes about poetry. His enthusiasm was contagious and his desire authentic. Soon men who never wrote a poem in their lives were sitting in his class and scorching paper with the power of their passionate words.

He acted on his vision of creating a space for men to develop and mature into healthy masculine fathers, husbands, sons, brothers. The space was created, nurtured, and blessed with men who shared his vision. He made these visions his mission in his short life, he made his time with us count by developing and using the gifts he was blessed and born with.

Patrick was impatient for prisoners to see and grasp his vision for the men's circles. He put in his own inner work and inspired us. We did not comprehend the significance of the healing and recovery process that he started until years later. By then it was too late to express our joyful and insightful experiences with him.

Patrick suffered from complications of hepatitis-C the entire time he was enrolling us in his program for our own benefit. He succumbed to this illness in April 2000.

Many of us try to sustain his vision by adopting it as our own. This book is a compilation of that effort and dedicated to Patrick Nolan, he was the inspiration and catalyst of it all...inside prison.

His legacy lives on and the impact of his tireless efforts has reached thousands. A lot of what is in the Folsom Prison Daybook, one way or the another is relatable to his energetic influence. With heartfelt thanks and deep, and intense gratitude we dedicate this book to one of the best of us—Patrick Nolan

Intention

We believe in the healing provided by
inspiration.

The words in these poems and writings are
representative of the ripples of inspiration on
waters of hope.

We pray that hearts are touched, minds are
provoked, and souls will sing.

These words are shared from meaningful places
touched by the authors.

May you find solace in the knowledge that
feelings were plumbed to find the ache of these
expressions.

—•—

Forward

POETRY AND THE BEGINNING OF THE CIRCLES INSIDE
By Don Morrison

As I approached age fifty in 1985, I had been through a costly divorce, was separated from my children, was dissatisfied with my career, and had started to ask, "is that all there is?" At the invitation of a friend, I went to a week-long gathering led by the poet Robert Bly in an old retreat center up in the Mendocino woodlands. I'd never read poetry, so never suspected that the answer to my question might be in poetry. But Bly scratched an itch I had not felt. I was unaware of the allure of poetry, but now I started to read and then to write poetry. By the fall of 1992, I was hooked on poetry, and one night lying in bed leafing through a magazine, I came across this stunning poem:

Little Monkey Man

He grips, between trembling hands wet with bath water,
a stiff bristle brush. He is six years old, and tears
run in rivulets down plum colored checks. With cleanser
he begins to scrub the soft black skin of his legs;
it hurts, but after awhile, the whitewashing numbs. He wants
to be clean, to never again worry about getting locked in
a cage. Sweat mixes the cleanser with blood; his tiny
frame spasms with frustration; his skin gets darker…
He never wants to hear again,
"He's a little monkey man," and "belongs in a cage,"
or at least that's what the white kids say.

The byline said: "Patrick Nolan, who is serving a life sentence in New Folsom Prison."

I was impressed. In my belated interest in poetry I had found there was a long tradition of good writing by prison poets. I was especially taken at that moment with the poetry of Etheridge Knight, a black poet who had started writing in prison. I had heard him read his poetry and knew there was something in the prison experience that touched me. This fellow Nolan tapped into that same vein of interest, and I made a mental note.

Then, a few weeks later in another magazine, I came across another of his poems and again I was touched. Again, the byline said, "Patrick Nolan, who is serving a life sentence in New Folsom Prison."

His poems had the same lack of self-pity and an acceptance of suffering that I found in Knight's poems. I assumed that Nolan like Knight must be black; especially after "Little Monkey Man," I assumed came from growing up black. How else do you come to such an acceptance of life's sorrow and heartache without pity or bitterness? I decided to write Nolan. I asked for a few of his poems and told him about Knight and asked if he knew of his work.

He responded with several of his own poems. Yes, he had heard of Knight, but did not have any of his poems. I sent him some of my favorite Knight poems. A regular correspondence ensued.

Finally, I summoned my courage and said that since I lived in Sacramento, and was thirty minutes from New Folsom Prison, I would consider an invitation to the prison for a visit. He sent me the necessary paperwork, and in a few weeks, I found myself confronting my fears as I worked my way through the scans, searches and other indignities of visiting an inmate in prison.

My first surprise was that Nolan was a tall white man, 6 foot 6 inches, with a heavyweight boxer's build—which he had been in his youth. He was what my father, a first-generation Irish American, would have called "black Irish." Dark, neatly cropped black hair, thick eyebrows, deeply recessed eyes and a deep emotional reserve. He rarely smiled and was careful to hide several broken teeth, due to accidents, fights, and neglect.

First, we talked poetry and our favorite poets. Due to prison rules, it was not possible for either of us to bring printed material to the visits. We could only send them to each other by mail. If I wanted to share a poem during a visit, I would have to memorize it. The Irish poet W.B. Yeats was a shared passion, and so I started memorizing Yeats.

The visits became a monthly ritual; first getting caught up on the details of life, my kids, my business, his prison job, his cell mates, etc. Then we'd turn to our writing; poetry, stories, and things we had read. We'd "feast" on cookies and candy bars and soda pop from the vending machines which lined the visiting room.

Due to my painful back, every hour or so, we'd take a break and do several laps counterclockwise around the circumference of the visiting room. It was during these walks that I'd share the memorized poems. There was something calming about walking; that let the cadence of the poetry come through.

Prior to meeting Nolan, while enthused by poetry and Knight and Bly, I'd become involved in "men's work." Out of those retreats came the idea of "men's groups," where men gathered weekly to sing, drum, chant and tell stories from their lives. I had joined such a group. The central benefit was hearing the stories of the men present, and the dawning realization that I was not alone. What I'd endured in silence was really a shared experience.

There were common themes that ran through our lives and, we learned, had run through men's lives for generations; an exasperating attraction to women, unfulfilling work, worry about our children's futures. I shared these experience of my men's groups with Nolan and gave him some of the texts that were important to the men in the groups: Tending the Fire, A Circle of Men, but most important an anthology of poems that spoke to these male themes; The Rag and Bone Shop of the Heart.

After several years of visits there was a race riot on B Yard at the prison. During the riot, a prisoner was killed. There followed a six-month "lockdown," where men were confined except for a weekly shower and were fed in their cells. I wrote to Nolan during the lockdown, and it was during this period of confinement that he determined that he would try and change the conditions of inmate life.

His chief effort was to start a "men's group," which he envisioned would include men of all races and religions and share the deepest elements of what it meant to be a man, especially in a maximum-security prison.

An unwritten rule of prison life is the division of men along race lines. There is much tension and conflict between the races over real and imagined incidents of 'disrespect' for breaking this rule.

An unspoken rule was that the prison chapel was one of the only places where men of different races could interact without violating this rule. Nolan enlisted the Catholic Chaplain, Dennis Merino, to help in forming the first group inside the chapel.

Nolan spent several months walking the track of B Yard, explaining his idea to individual men who he thought would make good candidates for his proposed group. He carefully selected men who had some "standing" or "juice" with other men in their racial group. He reasoned that if a leader of a racial group attended a multiracial group, he would not be under the same pressure to report what was happening as a lower level member of the group would experience.

At first most of the men he approached were skeptical or hostile, but he persisted and finally leaders from all three major groups agreed—black, white and Hispanic.

Because it was such a violation of prison rules to meet in a multiracial group, Chaplain Merino would go to the cell blocks after "count" and evening lockdown and call out the individuals and escort them to the chapel. Such a visit from the chaplain usually indicated a death or crisis in the family.

In this way the first Men's Support Group got started in secret. At first it was very low key, with just an exchange of names and hometowns and the barest details of their lives. Gradually as trust built, they delved deeper. At one of the later meetings, the challenge was to talk about their mothers—what was her name, what was she like, etc. One of the men resisted giving his mother's name, because as he explained, "If I know your mother's name, it makes it harder to kill you."

In this way, trust built slowly, because the men honored a primary agreement; "What's said and done here, stays here." As trust built that their secrets would not be violated, deeper work and sharing were possible. It's the trust and the depth of this work that give the groups their attraction and staying power.

I was on Nolan's visitor card and therefore ineligible to be a part of these circles in the chapel. Rob Allbee, a poet and friend from my men's circle in Sacramento, stepped up and volunteered to facilitate these new groups inside. As a former convict himself he knew prison culture and as a published poet was already teaching writing in the prison's Arts-in-Correction writing program.

While the groups gained momentum under Allbee's facilitation, Nolan and I continued visiting monthly. As poetry had been the touchstone at the beginning of our friendship, it became a staple of the group's routine. In the beginning, a participant would select at a poem from the Rag and Bone Shop of the Heart to open the circle. Gradually, poems written by the men in Allbee's writing classes, were also used to open the circle.

When the circles had been going for a year or two, Allbee organized a weekend retreat in the chapel modeled after the ManKind Project's "New Warrior Training Adventure." At the end of the weekend of sharing and deep work, men were gifted with a name that reflected their inner gifts, or their "medicine" and the antidote to their "poison." In the circles, thereafter, the men used this "spirit name" as an identifier.

The deep feeling generated in the circles, with Nolan's poetic example, produced an outpouring of poetry by the men as they reflected on these new feelings. These poems and reflective pieces were copied and handed around from man to man with the a "spirit name" as its author for the protection of the writer. Gradually these pieces were gathered into a rough compilation of sheets the men referred to as "The Anthology."

Finally, Bernard Gordon, the chapel clerk, with access to a computer, volunteered to edit this compilation of nearly a thousand pieces into a volume that would present a single piece for every day of the year; a "yearbook." The result of this labor is the book you hold in your hands.

What I discovered at the Bly retreat was not just the answer to my question; "Is that all there is?" There was "more, lots more, even beyond poetry" It led to a deep friendship with Nolan till his death from illness in 2000 and the flowering of poetry in the men, who like me, had not considered poetry and reflective writing as a golden thread into my heart. This book is a testament to Nolan's belief in poetry as an instrument for a man to find his "medicine" and to live his life from that core belief in himself.

Forward

A Welcome to the First Inside Circle

By Rob Allbee

My name is Rob Allbee / Lion that sometime catches fire. I want to tell you a little bit about how this training came about because it is an extension of my mission and vision.

First, though, let me thank you for stepping forward to support these men in prison. My experience with them says that they are coming to "work" and I know and expect that you will do the same.

About three years ago, Don Morrison and I were invited to talk about the ManKind Project to the Pre-Release Program at Folsom Prison. Some prisons offer this program to inmates who are about to parole. It is approximately 100 hours of instruction and information about programs available "on the street" to help the men get started with their lives again when they get out.

The Pre-Release Program coordinator at Folsom was Dr. Harvey Shrum. After hearing us describe the ManKind Project and the New Warrior Training several times, Dr. Shrum asked us to consider the possibility of offering a version of the program to prisoners serving longer sentences, including men doing life sentences.

Through a long chain of circumstance that I will not go into here, I had already been conducting several I-Group type circles in the companion prison to Folsom State Prison, which is known as New Folsom. I had always wondered about the possibility of doing a New Warrior type training on the inside.

When Dr. Shrum offered us a time and place in the old prison to conduct such a training inside the walls, I decided to "go for it." With a couple of Dr. Shrum's inmate clerks (both serving life sentences) as allies, we began to spread the word to the inmate population. Because I am an ex-convict and look like it, and because of my intensity for this work, we soon had a group of 20 men, many of them "lifers" with "yard clout" interested in participating. That was six months ago.

From the beginning, these men knew about this date in May 2000 and that is what they have been heading for. I have personally spent a lot of time and energy exploring the initiatory process. I talked with the men about men's work and what initiation is and is not. These men who have stayed with the group are serious about salvaging something of their lives. Some of them will never get out of prison. While a couple are under 40 most are in their 40's and 50's.

We have spent a lot of time building trust by gradually exploring their feelings about their day-to-day lives. We have encouraged them to take responsibility for their feelings.

We have started to teach the language of responsibility. We have introduced the idea of inviting spirit or their idea of a higher power into the work. These are very new concepts for them.

I am confident that come Monday, May 22, 2000 we will have 15 men ready to "work."

Table of Contents

Introduction

I don't know anyone who can completely describe all the aspects of prison life, even the men who have lived there for years. The poetry in this book captures these prison poet's impulses in vivid detail.

Two main concepts in this compilation are Prison Life and The Men's Support Group.

Men's Support Group was sacred space created by prisoners who are desperate for relief from the drudgery of their lives and their intense struggle to grow into the lives they were born to live. Those lives can only be discovered through self-exploration, acceptance, accountability, and forgiveness.

One of the poets described his own moments of awareness of Prison Life; "I played the game in the fast lane for ten years. What got me on my last trip to the hole was this; after ten years of playing this monster role, I was with the same dudes sitting in the hole year after year...the same dudes. I'd been doing this stupid shit with them for the last decade and they are still there.

I said to myself, "Enough is enough. I have not changed a damn thing and neither have they. I needed change, but before I can do that, I must make some pretty big changes in me. I know it's hard, it's real hard. I needed to see goodness in the dark and I was very dark. I do dark real well. This isn't what I want for my life and this is not what I want for those in my family who still give a shit about me in spite of how I acted and in spite of all the blood I have spilled.

The Men's Support Group started with "who the hell am I and what do I really want"? And let's not forget, do I like who I am? This was a real easy question for me. Hell no. I didn't like who I was. Then I had to ask myself, who do I want to be? And I didn't want to be a monster; that fucked me up. I mean I spent my whole life teaching myself how to be the perfect monster, how not to care, how to hide everything I felt and to hurt or kill anything that tested that. I became an active member of the Men's Support Group about eight years ago, nurturing and protecting the sacred spaces. In many instances this was a personally painful process that eventually found itself expressed in poetry. I needed to express some of the feelings I was experiencing during certain parts of my work, going on around me and inside me at different times about my evolution and growth; these feelings.

These feelings were basic to my growth experiences, and only a portion of the whole that I was experiencing at a given time. Poetry satisfied that need. All of it is glimpsed and the moments I felt one way or another journeying through my Shadowland and the Shadowland of my fellow Group members."

Two other poets describe their discovery of their gifts for words: "Some of my poetry is about my pain. Some of my poetry is also about looking at myself in the mirror and recognizing for a split second how ugly and broken I am…

There are also some poems I've written out of my own arrogance and malignant pride; my insecurities and wants. And very few about understanding and love. I can't say I see everything around me. I'm sure there are things I don't see, but the little I can, I try to transform into words for my own satisfaction, and lust for feelings; since on paper I can make what seems like giants look weak and small; as I see it.

"Also in my poetry, I can be who I truly am without leaving out any the gross details of the role I've played and am playing in life. "My words are mine…but I welcome anybody to read them and find what-ever meaning they can in them.

I found myself one day full of emotions I couldn't explain, so many feelings that were so old I thought were new.

All my life I was taught to keep shit inside, never knowing it was the very thing that held me back from growing.

I've been in hell all my life…I was sixteen when I fell into the clutches of iron fingers. A miraculous thing happened. I found a missing piece of myself in a pen and paper…in this sorrowful journey of mine as it continued, I became more distant from who I was, wearing one mask after another. After many years I had a thick layer of disguises wrapped up within my skin…Layers of my skin I am able to slowly peel away; many has shown itself repeatedly, but I hope you can see me through the garbage because these emotions are real. This is me the frustrated, angry, sad, lonely, mad, insane genius and retarded man inflicted with love, all living inside this hopeful mind.

These are the realities of prison life and the steps of a process (transformation) into a hoped-for life and the requirements necessary to stay transformed and grow.

Most of these poems were composed between 1997 and 2005. The word smithing is still going on and the transformations are continuing thanks to all the volunteers and the prisoners sick and tired of being sick and tired. Even among the walking dead, hope finds a way of growing and thriving in the hearts of those out of sight.

January – Month One

Paths, Searching, Seeking Life

The transformative path of introspection and self-discovery brings the unexpected, and sometimes surprise, shock, and wonder. Searching done in unfamiliar ways, and conditions, one is awkward and easily mislead or deceived.

Being a spectator to life's seeming casual events often brings profound experiences or even diversity of misery or surprising normalcy. At the end of life, one is left with the memories of tragedy and validation of its sanctity.

The labors along the path, means accepting it's reality, challenges, and consequences, often demanding courageous reactions. Driven by unnamed desires means being open to what happens.

The time takes a toll on life, the unwanted ones often not seen in plain sight, make up minor steps along the way. The restlessness of life and the unbearable waiting for destiny be revealed are tedious and the different meanings of a lifetime of waiting. There are many tests exposing our inadequacies and marveling at our strengths. At the end of life, who or what determines if it was a failure or success?

This

~

He was born to this he said often
born to these rules, these codes, to the prison face
the imprinted look of certain lines,
a certain geographical depth of eye-sockets,
a certain blankness of the eyes, like broken windows.
He was born to this by a mother's suicide,
a brutal father's drunken fist,
a world of howling lost boys scavenging in clubs,
in pockets, in veins,
embracing shadow and fallen-ness
and quick to break the fingers
of those who brought him here.

~ Shaman's Key ~

Time Wasted or Not

◈

Misplaced hope say most.
Some say I'm wasting my time.
Some say I'm wasting everybody' time.
But then these are the same voices
that told the ones
still left in my corner across the street,
watching from a safe distance, that I was well beyond repair.

I remember the tortured look on their faces,
the ones left watching and praying for me,
"He's gone. He's gone." and it was said
over and over in a million different ways.

Reflected off huge sheets of storefront window glass
off the shiny faces of the TV people
who have never felt
with bare skin cold sidewalk concrete
and off the sides of all the buses
off brilliant yellow summer dresses
off freshly painted orange bridges
high above the deep water
only seconds from the last stop ocean
and off the rich sounds of the women singing
their very souls, clean and true towards death.

But I made it to here
I still draw breath, hopeful breath
that I pass to my sons
and the ones
who they almost all say
are beyond, beyond.

~ Lion Who Sometime Catches Fire ~

Intruder

❧

A weary man is traveling in a forests
on his way to no place in particular.
He is carrying with him everything he owns,
including his visions and failures.
Inadvertently in the shadows,
he steps on a hidden branch that snaps
under his heavy weight
sending a loud crack
suddenly crashing out
into every corner of the forest.
He stops and everything stands there
frozen in the crack.
The rocks and the pines hold still.
The steam, tiny ferns,
a crow, red berries,
a wolf higher up,
even the sky stops and leans in a bit.
He is close…very close.

He looks around.
He moves on.
The stream continues on around the bend.
the ferns return to casting shadows.
A crow flies away.
He looks back once,
as he crosses the ridge.

~ Patrick Nolan ~

Could You Learn on an Empty Stomach

Running around trying to survive while pretendingto be clean and courteous wearing a costume to get you in the door where the food is plenty and the walls are cozy. You're not rich; you're not poor; you're just theretrying not to be noticed while also trying to fit in; could you feel love, compassion and trust on an empty stomach?

Your pains are not only of hunger…they're of a longing, of a weary tireless search of a place to belong to, for someone to understand and feel your pains, to love and care about you,where you don't have to wear the costume or worry aboutwhat you got to eat or if you'll be safe.

When you're hungry and not sure what tomorrow brings getting through today is the only thing important to you; it's not about having fun…it's never been about having fun.

When you're hungry you learn to do all the wrong things because doing the right things won't feed your stomach because doing the right things won't protect you from the scars you've already endured.

Could you think positive and see the good in others, trust and respect the adult figures that have already abandoned you?

Who would you turn to, where would you go, what would you do if you were hungry and didn't have anybody?

The dopeman gave me a rock…that first cloud of smoke?

I forgot about my hunger. When I was locked up that hunger was banished with a jailhouse knife and so-called "homie love."

I've been hungry all my life and when I got out to the streets I was still hungry. I traded my soul for a taste of animal flesh.

I often traded myself for just a little bit of warmth,food and a shower, always leaving my tastebuds unsated. My appetite became desperate and my search frantic: I still have no home and my hunger still exists.

I look back at an empty plate and vacant seats not knowing what a real meal consists of.

I would like to learn what you think: you have to teach, but not on an empty stomach.

What have you learned?

~ Patrick Nolan ~

In the City

❧

The blind man sings
swinging his can filled
with pencils.
He sings, people pass,
I stand to one side
and watch the scene.
Opposite the blind man,
a man in a red sweater ablaze
with buttons that quote biblical sayings
swears from his platform of milk-crates
that judgment day is on hand:
"Sinners be damned!"
I watch this display at a cross-roads
in my life—waiting for some sign
of destiny, or something, anyway.
At one corner,
across from where
the prophet screams his spittled flames,

a woman is pressed a crack
between two buildings, wrapped
in multi-colored scarves–she doesn't
move, she doesn't speak–just sits there
day after day woolly and obscure
to the traffic passing by.
This is culture in poverty,
a diversity of misery scoffed at, and oftentimes
swept under the cracks.
The blind man walks away, eventually
a couple quarters richer. The prophet
caught up in his zeal marches on the local
Scientology Center.
The woman remains where she is
until someone finally notices she is dead.

~ Patrick Nolan ~

Untitled

❧

It is all here, friend – the HIV patient
scratching like a junky jonesing
for a fix – body bags and toe tags –
and they drop like flies, two
and three a week…

Give me a poem that decries life's
tragedies
so I can appreciate life's inviolable
sanctity.

~ Patrick Nolan ~

Things Change

❧

Things change, such is the way of our existence. Beginnings start, middle pass, and ends rush headlong into us. My desire is to preserve some moments in my life into more than just memories and my desire etches on my souls glass a great thirst to live like I lived in those moments against because for one small increment in time and space the pain of just living life and the joy of being alive blended into some sweet elixir that we all drank and just "WERE" we "WERE." All of us present in the now and yesterday wasn't as heavy in my heart and tomorrow was far past my horizon and I wasn't alone there, I can't forget I saw you too. If in my travels down my path I forget the glory that was, yell at me, point your finger and scream I SAW YOU! SING MY SONG! Make it not an accusation that I was wrong to forget but that you must get my attention; and help push my inner-self into my heart space because when you do that; brother you save my life, you grab my arm as I stumble on my path, you; drag me away from the edges of the steep narrow trail we all are on; following it up, down and sideways at times. Do you grasp the seriousness of what I speak of brother? Do you fed in your heart my words are true?

Because if you doubt ask yourself when you wander off that path your on into your forest and far off you hear the voices screaming "I saw you", and your name is echoing forever towards you ask yourself are they calling you just because you are lost or is it that they are the voices of men you know what it means to leave the safety of a clear pathway to follow you; find you, and go with you wherever you go because they too were lost; and alone and forgot a moment in their lives until someone came after them and now they look for you to be with you and bring you back to your pathway not just because one of us go lost but because they know you; leave no one behind even though none of us can tell you where this path we are all on started or where it ends. I can only tell you that when you're on it with me the going gets easier and my footsteps fall more solidly to the ground and I don't feel so alone. This is what makes the journey bearable.

~ King Mongoose ~

To My Brothers

⌖

How can I say "I am" when my examples don't exist.
How can I say "I do" when my labor is void of sweat?
I am not one to dilude myself with imagination
and wishful thinking as I dance on the verge of reality.
I do not seek shelter from the storm of challenges
nor avoid the rain of their consequences.
Like you, I have been ordained to subvert ignorance,
harness stupidity, shadow deceit and let truth breath!
Like you, darkness has tempted me.
People whom we have a right to expect something from
fail us as we slowly fail ourselves
and shake our fists to the heavens and ask "why?"
I know this to be true because each and every one of you
are the large and small parts of me.
My journey has been your journey
and with sorrow and sadness
you have been my only companions.
I miss your laughter, your smiles, your hopes, your defeats
and even the victories that last only a short while.
But this void and this emptiness will not last long.
I shall be among you shortly
and I pray that I am worthy to be received.

~ Unknown ~

Not a Dream

~

In my dream time
My unconsciousness wanders to places, I dare not go
while awake…
Driven by the desire to find answers
To this never ending quest, called life.
Is it the truth of our nature
I really seek?
Or mere answers to this empty feeling
I carry?
But am too afraid to confess
to my awakened self.
Is there a cure to our demonic ways?
Or is it just another empty promise
of redemption?

~ Fierce Fox ~

4th Street San Rafael, 1983

❧

She ain't walking
gray cracked concrete picking through the cans
with strays and crazy pricks for her health.
This ain't her fucking lunchbreak.
It ain't a suntan;
It's wind and sun and old grease and new dirt
filling the cracked bland, eroded face, creeping beneath her clothes
to fester the unwashed legions
that once itched, then burned,
then became more intimate demons.
A thin cigar stays clenched between crooked teeth and lips
thinly trickling brown drool that smears her chin.
A heavy ski-cap with big fuzzy ball is pulled down past her ears,
blond tendrils cling wetly to forehead and cheeks.
She comes to me like a wounded ape,
bowlegged, limping, hunching ahead under long beige corduroy,
dazed colorless eyes welling with defensive tears
as she says - slurs - gargles
"give me money"
without humility or expectation
for she will have
or she won't have
there is no in-between.
I give her everything in my pockets;
a ten, a five, some change,
a pack of cigarettes
and I think I'm one hell'uva guy
as she walks her aching legs
down 4th Street.

~ Shamans Key ~

What I Know I Have

❧

Ask me what I'm doing and I'd say
Waiting–
Yes waiting.
Not for any eminent miracle,
but for that unreachable moment of peace of total rest.
Maybe I'm trying too hard to find that awaited dream.
It's so easy to do this waiting.
I have all the hours of day and night–
I can sit or sleep in waiting.
So don't blame me, all I have left
is this undeniable urge to wait…
My life has become a waiting puzzle.
I am a man now, not a boy of seventeen
but it doesn't matter if I live to be one hundred
I'll still be here wearing my waiting mask
so patiently plastered on my face.
I'll be counting left over souls
listening to their stories being told
by the old, or young–
I won't grow tired…
of the sour taste of our air
of days without the sound of clocks on the wall.
I'll be just waiting for my moment,
for a friendly smile to arrive
for God's loving arms
to finally embrace this broken down machine I've become.

~ Fierce Fox ~

An Envious Emotion

❧

AI envy you
You that life charms
with a sense of meaning.
I envy you
You that makes my one day
more meaningful than an entire life.
I envy-the wild beasts
and everything that holds no reason
but-it is reason itself.
How I envy those fools in love
Holding each other so tight,
for I've forgotten
The sweetness of a woman's touch.
The surrendering of my hearts soul.
I feast my eyes upon this enigma
Beholding the beauty of nature's life.
Unable to reach its core
I stand alone wondering,
if this tiresome path
My destiny way
forgotten.
Maybe-
If I let my eyes drift apart-
and roam on their own will
That light I seek
will be
finally found.

~ Fierce Fox ~

Within

ॐ

To go within you must first go without. For the way within is staked with pitfalls and traps. The dangers arise at every step of the journey and as the pressure increases to push the intruder back and expel him from the pathway and into some dark alcove where shadows can weave their web and overcome our hero. Our hero? The one who will stand against the forces of evil, smitten with a cause. Who will gloriously fall upon his own sword should the need arise. Our willing martyr and village idiot enamored with an ideal sense that he can make it right and save the world. Our villain, the shadow king, dark prince, essence of old, every childhood nightmare you've ever had embodied in one essence and possessing powers that supersede the hero's virtues. He stands against our hero, empowered with a lifetime of failures, mistakes, and inadequacies to hurl at our hero and knock him from his path.

Somewhere in the depths a climatic scene is brewing. The stage will be set, lighting chosen, and words chosen for the showdown. A battle both physical and mental will ensue where both sides will take to task the survival of a way of life.

~ King Mongoose ~

The Ocean of Sorrow

The pressure increases, I hold my breath and search for options, none. No air left, the surface more than a mile above, the edge of the abyss is cold. Why did I come here? I knew the risk. What did I expect to find? Desolation and shame. A lifeless dream-like landscape stares back at me, the intruder here, the silences echo. I look over the lip in desperation there's another bottom down there I can see it! I wasn't at the edge of something endless; I see another ground- what's there? Suddenly I feel myself floating up. I panic, my feet scramble for purchase I float and rise, it's like flight. I start to feel high and doped up. I blink in slow motion and everything is blurry, I look up through the inky blackness and see the orb of life shining on me even at this depth. I feel the eternal tug pull at my veins- is this my light at the end of the tunnel? I lose consciousness, pieces of reality drift by looking me in the face like strangers then racing away. I feel beating on my chest, I breathe deeply, it doesn't work. My body is numb, I push the water out, it races out my throat to leave, some shortcuts through my nostrils. It's out and the oxygen burns fiery trails into my lungs, they expand and contract. I see spots of red, yellow, and blue. My spectrum intact, I hear angels singing praise for life. I shake my head to clear my vision, candlelight registers and I focus in the pattern in the rug. I'm back from the depths.

~ King Mongoose ~

Untitled

❧

I wish I could help you help you with the load,
the thing, but it's like wishing I could help the Chileans
and the Cong, the fly-faced children
sucking dirt off their fingers
the boat people and the Afghans
and the shrieking napalmed eight-year-olds
and the Jews and the Gypsies and the heretics
and the old blind bluesman and the heroin freak
the palsied boy flinging his arms
the weeping mothers and impotent fathers
the freckled, fair-haired skinhead spitting on the cross
and Perpetua in the pit and Jeremiah in the pit
and me and you and them in the pit
and all the crucified all the hanged, the pierced
the heaps in graves
those that clawed the wall, those that starved in barns
those that trudged daily in barely shoed feet
and wait for trash day
for dimes and quarters
for shaking heads and averted eyes
and the innocent in boxes
the poets redeemed
the artists and singers
and broken-tongued writers and lovers,
the laughers and every hallowed son-of-a-bitch
and every deformed limping saint
and I wish I could help you
but even more
I wish I could help
me.

~ *Shaman's Key* ~

Untitled

❧

I came into the world knowing only three things:
hunger, a need to be held, and something to cry about.
Forty-one years later nothing has changed.
There's something in me frail and selfish,
something that only knows that it's hungry
or that it's alone
or that life hurts
and if you don't fit in there I can't use you.
I've heard the scream of a cat being mauled by a dog
and I remember thinking
'I know what you mean.'
But it was only the scream that I understood.
Every pet I've had said feed me, hold me, fix me.
Like every friend every lover
every stranger I sat with for more than ten minutes.
My dictionary has 600,000 words
that all mean
feed me, hold me, fix me.
The seven last words of Christ on the cross were:
feed me, hold me, fix me.
I love you means:
feed me, hold me, fix me,
and all the ads
all the religions promise to:
feed me, hold me, fix me.
I'm hungry
I'm alone
Life hurts.
I've known it all along.

~ Shaman's Key ~

Sincerity

☞

I question my sincerity to change, doubt stems from my familiarity with the way I was, that sense of arrogance and all of the positive things I thought I was. Thoughts askew and disheveled feeling are now the status of my being, emotions running wild beneath the facade of my mask. Ah my mask, that gleaming armor polished and impenetrable hanging on a trophy wall with my sword and shield. Now dust collectors or so I thought, how I long to wear it and have it caress my soul, my pride, my ego. Like a lost love it calls to me in my wakefulness and haunts my dreams like a childhood boogeyman. What is this strange fixation with my shadow? Am I a dark soul called by dark gods to mutter arcane words and blood sacrifice to appease their hunger? Or is it my hunger in my dark rituals that I embrace? I long to be more than what I am, I strive to be more than what I was, I struggle to understand what I will and have become.

~ King Mongoose ~

Questions and Answers

How can I write about beauty

When all around me there's only misery?
How can I write about the morning rain
When my window lacks a view?

So, Why
I keep drifting away—wondering
When hopelessness is so thick in the air?

Why do I keep searching
When all the doors around me are closed?

Why do I look towards a future
When I lack a present?

How can I escape the grip of my demons
When they dwell within me?

Why do I thrive to revive my inner child
When I'm the cause of his death?

Why is my search so complicated
When I'm living my destiny?

So Why
If I have all the answers
I keep searching for truths?…

~ Fierce Fox ~

All I Want

❧

I don't want to wait
For a heaven or hell.

I don't want
To live in my past.

I don't want
False hope for my future.

I don't want
Rare moments of happiness.

I don't want
An eternity if waiting.

All I want
Is a moment of clarity.

~ Fierce Fox ~

Seeking More Than I Found

❧

I am seeking more than I found
I want to find something
that can make me forget
I live in the pits of hell.

I am seeking a forgotten feeling.
I am on a soul saving search.
I look and look
but the bliss I seek evades me.
I find moments of joy,
and there are even times
I throw my head back and laugh like a madman.
And still the bliss evades me…
I am seeking more than I have found…

~ Painted King ~

Untitled Number Nine

I'm eating knowledge

like it's fruit.

You can't change me;

Only I have that control.

It's time I open up these vaults

find out who I pretend to be

is really me.

My whole life is a movie

only I can see;

I filtered out portions

for you to read.

~ Loving Leopard ~

Untitled

❧

Lashed to the wheel
with five hundred more
that daily turn the stone,
grinding
the days into sand,
the sand to dust,
his long shadow
dogs each striding step
from fence to chapel
beneath the watchful eyes
of suited watchdogs
and shaved, illustrated heads.

In his left hand
is Robert Bly, a hastily rolled cigarette
in his right.

Under a dark ridge
of contemplative bone
fading hazel eyes
regard his shadow
with descriptive heart
and though not his friend
he is quick to claim it
for his own.

~ *Shamans Key* ~

Yielbongura

❧

Freedom reigns, freedom reigns. The voice of many has cried from the depths of souls. Behind the many voices of young and old how?

To the many, the question of freedom screams in the silence of multitudes in souls, of the living who's hands bare the desperate unseen cries of blood that has dripped, spilled and dried to no avail freedom sought.

For the soul, yet it remains never quite fully understood in search (despite) it's hurt, freedom reigns, it reigns. It rules in sovereignty.

It fools the fool that I was; that I can be. But it never has fooled the hearts that sought it diligently, to live in it's bliss, where the lips of happiness kisses the seeking heart that it may be comforted and secured as it is Yielbongura; the thing that knowledge can't eat, who's lips may taste but not eat, in all the time of creation where freedom is sought with the harmony of all creatures who's relation strive in the spirit of love and harmony, seeking that possible, not so possible afterlife that is yet to be seen. Yet to be told by the voices of experience, by a god who possesses and holds the mysteries of life that conceivably has been kept on his plate of existence free from the covetousness appetite of knowledge that devours the sacred meaning of this complex and all, so present creation where lost searching and wondering mortals ache as I seek the daily bliss to sustain me till my last but first day of the afterlife which my faith and hope lies and thrives within my aching heart of freedom. Freedom sought in God by His Spirit lead by a love that surpasses knowledge so that it can't be eaten while nibbles and small tastes of betrayal, deception and harm inflicted seems to have eaten away portions of the body of life in me co-existing who's bones and marrow of truth keeps in strength to sustain us in the sanity of life's sacredness and security of feelings.

Feelings lost, feelings gained, of hurt and pain, feelings feared and denied, feelings of achievement and defeated feelings the thing that knowledge can't eat.

~ Courageus Tiger ~

Men at Work

❧

Ho, to my fellow Warriors
I got a little something I must let go.
A small contemplation,
a passing thought,
a welcomed freak show.
Those words are to myself,
but that would be lying
for I desire to share with folk that care,
if not let it float away as hot air.
Being overwhelmed with this,
I keep coming to the crossroads,
that leads to growth and healing.
But I come to a halt,
with that familiar feeling.
I escape quickly by focusing my eyes
on all the signs.

They read:

STOP, DEAD END, NOT A THROUGH STREET,
CAUTION, REST STOP,
CHILDREN AT PLAY, and ONE-WAY.

All those basic road signs speak so clearly also on a spiritual plain.
If you get my meaning, deep within the Circle.
All alone with no real men to travel along my side.
I get so twisted, confused and destructive in foolish pride.
There's hope for me here yet.
For I have experienced, seen and felt it all around, so real,
so true inside of me, inside of you.
Through all these cobwebs, I've woven to confusion.
I can see a very wise and good sign, that I can honor and respect
In this moment, at these crossroads in my life,
it powerfully reads:
MEN AT WORK!

~ Young Stallion — The Chosen Son ~

What's It Means

~~

The confusion was so thick, the meaning so vague.
I had to be wise to understand
and I was too young to be wise.
Filled was I with passionate unanswered questions
that left me angry and utterly lost.
Adults around me gave me
half-assed answers with half hearted effort
their puffed up importance was all about a job title.
This is what it all means to them
I was still a spectator
watching men fighting to find their place in life
with smiles of relief about being accepted
Smiles that hide the dread of rejection
and painful anguish of not belonging.
This meaninglessness wasn't for me
I needed more
but I couldn't
find more
I became cynical and sarcastic
unfilled and left searching.
It wasn't money
It wasn't things
It wasn't a job
It wasn't people
not the people I knew
I knew what it was not
but I didn't know what it was…

~ Healing Wolf ~

Untitled Number Twenty

*

As I sit here with my fellow travelers
I watch the flame of the candle
Dancing and flickering
It mesmerizes me
Calms me
I feel my soul relax
I let my barriers cease to be
I feel
I soak up the peace that surrounds me
I'm not alone anymore
My pain, my fear
Comes through my mask of shame
I no longer hide
I welcome my truest feelings
I know I'm alive
Because I feel
I love.

~ Loving Leopard ~

It Started From–No

Our patron asked'em and he said, No!.
He said, men in prison can't do it
Their walls are way too high,
unyielding and strong
Severely dangerous they are too.

Another one of those " it couldn't be done" answers.
Prisoners can't reach that deep, it's too hard.
Prisoners can't feel that intense,

their hearts are badly broken and too neglected.
What the hell do prisoners do with their secret feelings
if the rare Clowns who know refuse their plea?
Our patron wouldn't accept these denials
so he nudged the Clown now and again,

until he said–Yes.
Now the Clown won't quit coming.
Now he says he's here as long as they let him.
Week after week he gets out of his sick bed.
Poor soul he's miserable as a wretch.
The Clown understands our need and his
and it too try's to kill him;
he shrugs it off and refuses to quit.

Now our Circle keeps feeding his soul,
keeping love alive,
and our Clown,
and our hope…

~ Healing Wolf ~

Passionate Compassion

～

I'm wounded and I suffer with these wounds.
This suffering is very painful.
These wounds cover every inch of my body…
My wounds are emotional wounds
Invisible to casual observation…
Some in my Circle of Sanctuary are very aware of my wounds,
and are sympathetic, with the intention of alleviating my pain.

The Circle has medicine,
I come to my Sanctuary seeking medicine,
To ease my suffering and to heal…
To me this is compassion…
Everyone I know is suffering these wounds
with poisonous puss dripping from them…
And some times their puss drips into my wounds, infecting my wounds
with their poison,
Which eats away at my compassion, contaminating my medicine…

Only the power of truth can keep my medicine
purified enough for compassion to nurture it's growth…
I need passionate compassion to heal my wounds…
I need passionate compassion to fight the poison…
I need passionate compassion
to see every one else's wounds, pain and puss.

~ Healing Wolf ~

Untitled

Moments of silence-of violence with nowhere to go, but to grow.
Since no choices are given and living everyday writing on paper with pen
discovering my thoughts of violence with no tolerance, over and over,
Day after day doing the same thing.
Nothing gets old for me, and it doesn't matter 'cause I'm a chatter who
carves; who arises to discover the betrayer, lover and hater. Who portrays
the glossy indistinct scenes Scenarios to everyone of my stories of the
streets.
I can play all day long, but no good will it do but'll mark me to stay stuck,
Abandoned to suffer to some story I can't rewind, good moments and
so fortunate I am; sitting next to Warriors that know the path, I played
and ran. I've walked in sorrows and despairs; I cried, hit, stole and use,
but today I chose to kill that part of my past and walk as a true blue
Warrior. Battling for the win-within with nothing to brag but embrace
around the truth. To see the next day. Many feelings come my way, with
not a single lie to say. Some fear death, some fear the worst, but I run,
hunt for good and bad; thus I don't, and won't allow, to follow another
fear, but stay real. To the game of death and living we all play.
In plans of death alone, my mind sometimes bleeds to death.
I played in the past too much everyday that nothing much was there, but
took me away, far away to the unfair.
I played risking my way of life;
I won, fought and lost, and nothing much was there but sadness and agony.
For all the pain I brought to one now I ask who won?

~ Significant Elk Who Soars ~

Words

~

I want to find words that are a balm to long ago inflicted wounds.
I want to find whole clusters of words that will heal
scars to the soul.
No words exist and no pretty sounds will ever erase what time and man
has done.
Maybe there is hope that words can some how wake up a feeling.
A feeling that we have all seemed to have lost.
A feeling a tiny little feeling that given a chance
will change the way we move across mother earth.
When I was born I came to this world un-afraid, trusting,
amazed by everything. I was love…
Tell me what words will give me that back?
I do not care about formats and proper wordage.
I want to be amazed by the sunlight on a stone wall.
I want to touch a long forgotten sacred part of who I am.
I want the sacred in you to talk to the sacred in me.
I can care less what words we use.
Maybe no words at all.
Let's be lights. Let's be real and move right past
pretty words and useless words like
color, race, religion, convict, free person.
We are all just humans trying to be strong.
But only in a human way.
Let's be god's. Let's be lights.
Let's be the power of change, let's be love.
Let's be what we were created to be.
What words do you know
that will help us be that?
I want to find them words.

~ *Painted King* ~

Doing the Hard Thing

❧

So I sit and I look at who it is I want to
some day become.
I want to become the man who knows how to help.
The man who can and will step outside what he
thinks is
safe and do the hard to do things.
so I sit here and write about the things I want to some day do
because that is so much easier than
getting off my ass and
doing them.
And tell me my good brothers
Just what the hell is it that needs doing?
What is it that you are missing in your life?
And what are you doing to change them?
Who do you some day want to become?
What are you doing to get there?
Are you just sitting there writing about them?
Or are you stepping
beyond what you feel is safe
and doing them?
How do I face the things
that hold me back?
what can I do to find out
what they are?
and once I find that out,
what will
I be brave enough to do

~ Painted King ~

February – Month Two

LAMENTING, GRIEF, SPIRITUAL

There are many ways in which we meet spirituality, some unexpected and most unfamiliar.

Poets' claim that life's sorrows bruise the indestructible soul, and it becomes strung out on life's sadness, regrets and pain.

Mystics confirm that only the body suffers life's indignities, never the pure glorified spark of God we proclaim as our soul.

But all agree that the twisting agony and tears pierce and darken the fragile human heart. Often the destruction is irreparable; marked by cold statues, head stones, graves, and rock gardens called cemeteries.

We are stuck in bodies that don't know what to do but react to what's done to it. Sympathetic wailings, evil emotions, pain, death, and shameful events. Sometimes these sorrows are locked in our memories with terrible clarity, often hunting us in our dreams.

We also have a different side to our spiritual natures; they leave the power of God's love alive in our hearts sustaining us during our darkest times.

This part of the book primarily deals with lamenting, grief and spirituality. The wonderfully descriptive language may even tug a few cords in the hardest of readers hearts.

The Other

～

Not me, not me,
but the other whose steps are not so loud
that lives in rooms with dark doors
down halls in rooms with dark doors
down halls where I lose my way,
and uplifts what I knock down;
who walks through walls
to view the unsheltered world
and who will stand my ground
when I myself am earth.

~ Unknown ~

What is Religion

～

Does a man have to be in a certain place,
For spirits to fly and hearts to race?
Does he have to look, dress, or act a certain way?
In order to sing and dance or receive the blessings of a New day?
Does he have to stand on a mountain top
And pray to the heavens above?
Or could it be something as simple as,
A gesture, a word, or a hand to someone you love?
Does it have to happen during Spring, Summer, Winter or Fall?
And is it necessary for him,
To get on his hands and knees and crawl?
Does he have to belong to a certain religion, race, color, or creed?
Or is it good enough that he is a man and the magic he believes?
Does he have to have a name like,
God, Allah, Buddha, Tunkashila, Jesus or Creator?
Or could His name be something as
common as Mother Nature?
Does He have to have a label like;
Pentecostal, Christian, Catholic, Islamic, Buddhism, Jewish, Jehovah, Red
Road or Baptist?
Or could the truth be that the message has long been missed?
Does a man really have to be in a Church, Chapel, Temple, Synagogue,
Sweatlodge or Mass?
Or could it be anywhere a Circle of men come
Who's souls have become lost?
Does a man really have to be in a certain place,
For spirits to fly and hearts to race?

~ Indio ~

Untitled

❧

Sadness comes…
When parting with someone…
You truly love…
When you're shocked…
By the loneliness…
In the absence…Of the one…
Who means…So much
When you're lost in thought…
Reliving moments…Spent together…
Before your parting
When longing…Tears at the fabric…
Of your being
Leaving you…In silent protest…
Beckoning…From the emptiness within…
the haunted chambers…
of your soul
Where the echoes…Of your beckoning…
Return…to a deepened…
Sense of loss…
That…My friend…Is sadness!!!

~ Soul Chamber ~

Untitled

❧

No longer do we refer to our teachers as fathers-
brothers are now foes to be wary of
and warred upon.

The simple symbolic references
have become dulled
in the reverence they once contained.
I hang my head in sorrow,
in shame, and silently grieve:
I want to cry,
to wail my misery
and aloneness to the wind,
but no one ever taught me:

My pain, my pain
Ah, the pain,
and the Great Spirit
now dust on a road no longer traveled:

I want to pray,
but don't know how,
nor can I sing without songs to praise
having fallen from the road into a grave
with all the teachers
I die.

~ Patrick Nolan ~

The Walk

❧

You have sent your child up
The dusty path many spring and summer times.
With clean white sheets
That your tears have fallen on,
That remind you who stand around a burning cross.
Up the dusty road that
You and your husband once walked on,
Taking back the clean sheets
To the white people
Who live up the dusty road.

~ Dusty Husband ~

Inside

❧

My life has been filled with so much sadness and despair
that as I walk down this road,
I find myself without emotion though it may be my life I am living,
I still find it unfamiliar.
How I have longed to have one to relate with
to trust to love with all of my soul and mind.

For you to be involved in my life
I will put you through a series of tests.
I must do all that I can to ensure that you love
in all circumstance for in my world there is only purity,
truth, respect and unconditional love.

This must not waiver from completeness
nor shall I be the enforcer to hold you true.
The one part of my world unknown to you
must be discovered by you.
I cannot assist you in your discovery
nor will I give you a clue
as to how to enter into it.
All of the answers must come from you.

What you desire may be yours
if you seek thoroughly
for in my world we are one.

~ Unknown ~

What It Is

❦

This ain't hell.
Even caves breed bats.
Even under cities things breed in the dark;
rats and disease that feed in rivers of human waste
beneath a concrete veil
of clean-swept streets
and pretty pastel houses all in a row.
And this ain't hell.
This is just concrete.
This is just water under a bridge,
a notch in the wrist, a scar, a cum-soaked sock,
a hiss in the night when afraid of death.
It's just a letter unwritten,
unsaid words like love, like later,
like "Sorry God."
Just a splinter in the eye, free to go mad,
free to chew my leg bloody 'cause
I can't drag the trap no more.

It's just teeth rotting, blood in the stool
the apathetic noose that hangs me every day;
the sins of the father,
every nouveau guru saying
"do this, read that, you're on the right road but your walk's all wrong."
It's just Jung and the Devil and Who failed Who
while the Lamb of God
points with wounded eyes
"when I sing" prayers in Celtic blues,
and eat his chalky bits of skin.
It's just a poet on the toilet
getting fucked by the needle,
the wrong ride when you're hitchin'
a child in the trash;
but this ain't hell.
this is just the way it is.

~ Shaman's Key ~

Untitled Number One

❧

I would have gladly borne him on my shoulders
all in raven and sables
measuring my steps with each beat of the dirge
while dismal April rained.
We'd have set him on barks
of damp rough cut pine still green
bowed our heads at pressed laments
and let the heart's black river flow;
beneath the biting damp gray
upon his mother's hill
I'd have worked the spade myself,
wept and sang and after,
drank myself to blindness.

But far and away
I hear of cardboard and ashes,
of wolves hair and my old blue knit cap,
a Canadian nickel and Celtic cross
and store bought prison blues,
no one to watch the strange, indifferent inferno
swallow him whole one last time.

~ Shamans Key ~

Emptiness

❧

I wish I could write a sad poem
that would let you feel the sadness
I sometimes feel,
and if I could
what good would it do?
Who would it help?

Who could it help?

Would it make my sadness any less?
No, I thought not
because you know and I know that sadness
that has grown this big
and has gone un-cared for this long
just can't be killed.

So I will live with the emptiness
that has become such a big part of my empty life.
And I will keep trying to write a poem
that makes me feel less empty…

~ Unknown ~

Untitled Number Two

⇟

I've chained it.
I bricked it up in walls.
I've tied it in a sack
    and thrown it in the river
    the ocean
    bottomless pits.
I left it in the woods to die.
I left it in the ghetto to die.
I left it on an ice flow
    with a pile of sticks
    when wolves were near.
I've rebuked it in the name of Christ.
I waved incense at it.
I had a priest and flock of holy crows
    dance it out in the Roman night.
I've had the fists of brothers
    pound it out,
    had it pounded out
    on djembes and congas
    and my skull by lathed limbs.
I burned it at the stake.
I buried it with the dead.
Gave it a life sentence.
I called it Darkness.
I called it Death.
I called it Shadow and Satan
    and the sins of the Father.
It's the only thing
about me
that's still holy.

~ Shamans Key ~

The Fifth Element

I am stretched along my past.
Deeply buried are my bones
hidden away from the ravenous wolves.
The world as I know it turns a blind eye.
Touch my tears before they evaporate into stains.
They fall ever so rarely.
She who sits still,
be still within these August days.
Let us dream within our silence
and look upon the sun
as it sets deep into our souls.
It shall rise once more stretching across my plains
and into the deep valleys of your heart.
Rummage through my broken past
and you'll find the missing pieces in a mirror.
Surely I was cut in four,
staked on a flag post
and placed at the far corners of this world.
My fifth element was placed in you.

~ Dancing Cobra ~

In the Chaos That Lives Within

&

In the chaos
that has become my life
I dive in self pity.
My soul
has fell victim
to my own demise.
Pride surrounds
me like an ocean.
Days to come
are not but mere reminders
of my present.
Love
is not but, just a thought of weakness…
Tears, if only I could make them disappear.
No one really knows
the language of our souls.
Too many conclusions have blocked our vision…
A vision of pure humanity.
I alone, don't stand blameless-
I alone hold responsibility
for the destruction
of that pureness in humanity.
Let someone be the judge,
and spare me no pain
because I alone have mutilated my own soul.

~ Fierce Fox ~

For the Sensitive Poet

❧

Some poets slay me
the way words tremble from their lips
like beads of rain off a leafy branch

And then there is melancholy crooner;
fragile as a porcelain tea cup painted sky blue,
with maybe a swan or crane
dipping in the backdrop.
So much sensitivity.
the bruised soul;
the jilted lover.
All that syrup sweetness
makes me sick after awhile.

Poetry isn't a game or leisurely pasttime.
People are dying from hunger—
ever see a man down on all fours
puking up his liver?
Or the look on the face
of a man attached to an oxygen tank
gasping like a fish out of water
because he only has a quarter piece of lung left?

It is all here, friend—the HIV patient
scratching like a junky jonesing for a fix—
body bags and toe tags—
and they drop like flies,
two and three a week.

So save all that "poor me, baby" shit.
Give me a poem that decries life's tragedies
so I can appreciate life's inviolable sanctity.

~ Patrick Nolan ~

Lost Childhood

<small>❧</small>

A small blue eyed child of three looks up at me
I feel the pride in my heart to know
that for the rest of my life I get to be his dad.

I got plans on how I am going to build him his
first bike, his first motorcycle; his first car
hell, who knows, I love him so much
I may even build him his first house.

I get to watch this beautiful child
live a joyful childhood.
I get to be his dad for the rest of my life.

That was then but this is now
I did not build his first bike
I did not build his first motorcycle
I did not build his first car
and I sure as hell did not
build his first house.

He is no longer a blue eyed child of three
and he no longer looks up at me.
I will carry with me the shame
in knowing that for the rest of my life I will be the
the dad that shattered his childhood.

For the rest of my life I will be his dad.

~ Painted King ~

Not I

*

Never have I been I,
but he who is forever in the shadow.
He sleeps and awakes in dark crevices and,
somehow I always managed to remember.
He sit lurkingly, motionless,
and serene seething with hate.
But I forgive him and love him,
still he creeps in the night
and I forever in the way.
And in-between that divided light,
I have lived and died,
buried under he who seeks eternal death.

~ Dancing Cobra ~

Life...Am I Lying?

The journey of life is so complex in all it's beauty and deceit, from the moment we are ejected from the sanctuary of the womb to the last breath taken when death is knocking.

Anger, hate, disappointment...all lies! Everything. Nothing. It matters not. What matters but me. Myself?

Who am I. What will I become when my soul leaves the prison I am?

Defeat is the outcome I've chosen, lost in loneliness and dark despair.

I've cried instead of laughing; I've laughed when I wanted to cry.

All lies! What do I have. Who do I give it to?

Why do they deserve it. I've worked hard for my bittersweet anguish.

I'll not give it up unless something worthwhile is shown to occupy my hate. I want to know my hate; Why I carry it around like I would carry a baby. Protection. And merciless anger if threatened. Life. Whose is it. Certainly not mine. I don't want it, yet I have it.

Blessed for what. Lonely nights. Happy memories?

Memories. Don't patronize! Life. Erase the 'f' and you've got lie.

One I have to live everyday.

Look out my window to razor and wire and gun tower.

Fuckin' lies. I'm tired of it. When does it end?

When do I end it. I'll never give up.

But on what. Everything accomplished will not go with me to the other world. I don't need it. So forget it. I want to see the beauty others see. But it hides. All I see is fruitless despair. Dead hope. Withered faith and mortal hate. All around. Why am I writing this. I'm scared. And mad.

Hope is dead. It died long ago for me. Who can help. Why do you...or you...or you keep going. Where do you go when you sleep. What does your mind see. Want to know what mine sees. It sees death. Rotting death smelling, stinking, rotting death. Nothing. I have endless anger, so I'll quit. Look at my eyes; do you see pain. Do you see hurt. Anger?

Do I hide it well. Am I lying?

~ Unknown ~

Tomb Stone

❧

Gnarled roots like fingers splayed across the fields of cemetery
plots underneath dirt of dead children.
Marbled tombs of bleeding angels, Kissed by the breath of God
stars motionless pleading with heaven.
I walk lightly, my footsteps crushing the dry twigs and fallen
leaves.
I am halted by a raven perched on a headstone, silently watching.
Its black eyes like burning coal seem to pierce through my
flesh and understand why my heart bleeds.
I could feel the tiny hairs on my body stand like pin pricks and
the trembling waves of my skin as I struggle to
control my tear ducts.
Wonderful faces I witness from afar,
a lost child seeking refuge and answer in the fields of gray.
A little breeze of wind catches my tear on an autumn maple leaf,
it's tiny reflection holding happy memories.
I would sit under this enormous tree for hours,
a lone figure in it's shadow, frozen like a statue seeing
these vast plots, wondering will I get any visitors when I am
dead and gone…

~ Dancing Cobra ~

A Day of Mourning

❧

One morning wrenching cries came wailing, splitting through the
somber air. My heart constricted, twisted with agony.
Dry heaves from my chest and my air ways were slowly cut from my
esophagus. I don't know how but I managed to breathe.
I remember a boy with his tears straining to fall
as the windows are rolled down in the old family station wagon.
The tears that managed to escape from its prison
were pressed against his cheeks by the blowing breeze.
Somehow it felt the car was crying shaking its metal built body,
as it races along the tar pits and loose bits of gravel, flying and piercing
through the morbid air. I wonder if the pebbles hit the nearby pedestrians
or the kids who were playing on the sidewalk?
Maybe I will never know, we went by too quickly.
I do know when those sliding doors of death opened the place became
a mutated sanctuary. Its molecules split and forever changed its ideal for
me. I saw men and women with blue masks with god-like tendencies
stride in hurried steps. It felt like an infernal hell
as blood curdling cries tear through my already torn heart.

I cautiously walk, unease with each step as if the tiles underneath me
would soon crumble upon my soles.
My eyes squinting to see through building tears
and my ears screaming to hear
the dull blurry voices of softly padded footsteps
and the whispered monotone of consoling voices wrapped with
sympathy and compassion.
All the while,
I a zombie, aware of everything and nothing.
I glided along the last turn of corridors
and entered this strange and unearthly place
and saw merciless death claiming my beloved Grandma.

Dedicated to my beloved Grandma
I Love You Always.

~ Dancing Cobra ~

The Specials

≈

We call ourselves
The human race
But there are others amongst us
Those, I'd rather call "the Specials."
They see what no one can see
They hear with clarity
What we call noise
They smell all the parts of life
When they speak,
Our mind stops to listen.
Who are these beautiful beings?
Where have they come from?
We even have made names for them
Lamas, wisemen, medicine men,
Pastors, shaman; some even
Monsters, devils, demons
Weren't they borne from a woman as I?
And though cursed with our human form
They've blessed with eternal bliss…
I've felt their presence around me and
If I could ask for another life
I'd gladly be
A servant to their needs.

~ Fierce Fox ~

War and Peace

*

I pray for the day till my pain is eased,
Till then I war in rage,
Till death becomes my peace.
My heart, body, soul and mind feels the same pain;
This hell on earth.
I feel the flames of torture having been cursed since birth.
My suffering and misery exceeds the limit of life.
Still I breathe in death,
Living in anger and strife.
So I hope to be free one day from this pain I feel.
Till then I live in torture;
Till the darkness becomes real.
"My Eternal Conflict"

~ Dancing Cobra ~

Untitled

❧

I can't change it.
I can't change that I lost my wife and child
to time handed to me by a judge and my own crimes.

I can't change.
I watch my friends beat themselves down with "maybes"
and "what ifs"
fearing something that may never come.

And I can't change that I want to make a change.
I can't change the fucked up
empty, sad feeling I get
when I have to hang up the phone
or when I have to watch someone I love
walk out of the prison visiting room.

But I have to make myself change
or all this shit I can't change
will drive me insane.

~ Painted King ~

Untitled Number Fourteen

❧

I wish I was the special man
that's holding your hand
Tucking you in bed on a stormy night
there when your dreams turn bad
when you were scared of the night
crying out for me, only I'm not there.
I was far from you,
the days were few and far between
that we enjoyed each others company
even though this is true
it doesn't mean you were far from my heart.
I sat and cried on your birthdays
Christmas and any holidays you imagine.
Now as you grow older
I hope your heart doesn't grow
colder to wards me
Needing guidance, answers to your questions.
None of this is your fault.
I hold that burden on my shoulders.
Child, as you grow older
I hope you understand these words.
Most of all, I'm sorry.

~ Loving Leopard ~

Too Soon

❦

I over heard an angel speaking
whispering your name
His words floated on the wind
I only heard fragments of his message
He said you were safe and no longer in pain
I opened my eyes
tears streaming down my face
I cried out to God
Why him O Lord
I had so much to tell him
I've asked myself so many times
since you've left
were you scared
Who was holding your hand
as you took your last breath
I've closed my eyes now
I can see your face, I hear your voice
it's etched into my memory forever
I pray to God every night
that when it's my turn to go
I go to heaven
I have a few words to say
You left way too soon for me to tell you
I love you
I love you Dad.

~ Loving Leopard ~

Untitled Number Seven

Even though he's gone

angels by his side

know God's right there

His love still remains in all of us

He's better off now – no more pain

So don't cry – dry those eyes

He's still with us everyday

looking down on us with a smile

His laughter on the wind

living on through us – in our memories

to guide us – protect us

In his own special way

Just keep on loving him the same.

~ Loving Leopard ~

Patrick's Song

All the times I needed your blessing
Too weak to stand from raising the shield
Down on my knees but never confessing
That I was the one refusing to yield

Tell me why
Though I look at the wound in your eyes
I can't say what I feel
The way
That it's all up to you
Wraps my heart up in darkness
and breaks it in two

And I'd go with you to the top of the mountain
Sit through the storm at the heart of the sea
Fall like rain, drink from the fountain
Anyway or where you need me to be

Tell me why
though I look at the wound in your eyes
I can't say what I feel
The way
That it's all up to you
Wraps my heart up in darkness
and breaks it in two

~ Shamans Key ~

A Far Country

.๛

Far north
beyond wooded mountains
where the land slips
back into the sea;
rugged bay lines and frigid,
pale-gray coasts of Old World faces;
the shimmer of town lights on the inlet waters
like blue and yellow stars;
cold mornings turning stony cheekbones red
and frosting the breath as steel skates slide;
well-dressed poor boys hustling Toronto,
whores and needles and chipped tooth grins,
tears of ice weeping from downtown Mission eaves
like swords of Damocles
above the shivering sidewalk damned...

But he is in a far country
where it's not so sad to die,
but to die so far from home.
The words are the same
but alien on these southern tongues.
Fifteen years in twenty different tombs
of sterile gray
as the north turns it's back
on it's native, singing son,
until even the grave
of the mother he loves
no longer speaks.

~ *Shamans Key* ~

The Minstrel

❧

I have this old guitar with a ripped and ragged sheath. With honest work she's paid for, but stolen by a thief. She's got these marks on her but still she plays. All right and in these marks you'll find the story of my life.

I learned a lesson through restrained and bitter tears. In the summer of my adolescent years. Do not lie to those whose trust you should not betray. For in the end it all comes back to you one day. I was a minstrel I was a traveling wayfarer's song. I sang for you my tale of life. And then I was gone. Her hair was darker than the ebony of night. Her way was graceful as the grace of birds in flight. Her love was truer than the truest odes of rhyme. And such eternity made all commitments blind. In love there is weakness, in sorrow there is shame. And all can leave you weeping in the January rain. She found the strength one night to finally break away. She has my prayers but where she is I couldn't say. For I was a minstrel, I was a traveling wayfarer's song. I sang for you my tale of life, and then I was gone. Sweet sacrifices I made in love's name. Echo a lifetime of dreams spent in vain. The sweet caress of sunshine and passions lying flame.

Have left for me a legacy for which I accept all blame. Faces I have come to know, they tease my memory. A thousand nameless friendships that will never set me free. With God my superstition, with music as my truth, It left a scar upon me that one day I'll call my youth. And I was a minstrel I was a traveling wayfarer's song. I sang for you my tale of life, and then I was gone. Dusty are the countless roads I have traveled on. None have gone as far, as I, to hear my own song. I played the music sweetly, I played the music cruel, I called myself a minstrel.

Though you'd call me a fool.

~ Shamans Key ~

It Ain't Easy

❧

It ain't easy being who you can't be
It ain't easy gathering thoughts of death or living
It ain't easy obligating people to follow your doctrine
It ain't easy desiring the thing I want and need, but will not get
It ain't easy trusting when I've been deceived
It ain't easy getting where you want to get
It ain't easy living in peace
It ain't easy living the way I do when I deserve better
It ain't easy representing what you can't fulfill
It ain't easy escaping when lies are given
It ain't easy having what you can't replace…and
It ain't easy being good when this fucked up government
is falsely accusing the innocent
It ain't easy believing in Jesus Christ when his people are
full of contradictions, destruction and thieves…
It ain't easy believing in Jesus
when all his shit is all tangled up and full of lies
It ain't easy being a writer, and rider till death
It ain't easy bleeding your fingers to write about this shit.

~ Significant Elk Who Soars ~

Still I Think I Love Her

☙

Dreams, hopes and plans all so carelessly tossed aside.
Promises long forgotten by the ones who made them:
conversations fall apart even before the first word is uttered.
And still I think I love her:
Yesterday is long gone
tomorrow is only a hope.
Today is anger, loneliness, disappointment, rejection
and maybe even a small degree of hate.
And still I think I love her.

~ Painted King ~

March - Month Three

Awakening, Realization, Bonding, Awareness, Awakening

There's a word being used frequently to describe an unlimited amount of unnecessary thoughtlessness; it's called "unconsciousness." The many people going through life unconscious of the impact of their actions, words and behaviors is frightening. The time each of us spends "unconscious" is individual and cannot be predicted. The unspoken expectation is that something, somehow, someway will wake us up and we can start being "conscious" and living our lives as 'intentionally conscious.' Unfortunately, this isn't the way it works for most of us.

It's not that we don't want to live "conscious lives." Life happened to us before we even got our bearings of who and where we are in this beautiful mystery. We just started trying to react, learning how to survive.

All paths are interwoven, past, present and future, woven one inside the other and upon "awakening" we start to go back; but sometimes there are great distances in-between the occurrence of these conscious moments.

This awakening can mean stepping out of darkness, pain and poison and stepping into the illumination of medicine and healing. Learning to see wounds hidden in the deep past. The interior-self travels back and forth through time; and rising out of the ashes and old scabs, eager to reconnect to the beautiful language of being us.

This is only the turning point, this "awakening." Often this experience is intense that begins in confusion; an embarrassed surprise that happened when we were too young to do anything about it. We were too little to understand; choking at key times that changed life as we knew it. Stuck in the present, but eager to reconnect to the past. The differences that make us the same.

Opening "myself-to-myself" and understanding what I truly am. Like a reminiscing ghost only you can see, knowing everyone is as fucked as me. Stalking fear into the great 'unknowns' that reside within. Often, we bring our pains to those who care to try to unlive our lies, realizing our needs dictated our perceptions and wounds inflicted upon our ability to change and grow. They were forged from years of pain, sorrow, and sadness.

Evolution of Majesty

~

Unable to moun t my throne
my king weighted with poison
my will twisted with despair
the court infested with my shadows
darkening my medicine
heatedly criticizing & ejecting all who oppose me
dominated by self righteous venom
disconnected from my heart
I force my heart into the void
without facing the wrath I inflict on others
suffering the damned without medicine
I'm tired of the stench of festering wounds
aching to come out of the dark
fighting with dread and fear
I step into the Circle
beginning the journey to find the light
that heals and illuminates my throne
I was originally crowned to sit.

~ Healing Wolf ~

My Circles

Sitting in a tortured feeling of misplaced anger that's so.
It's hotter than the flame of anticipation of freedom
my lost spirit so desperately yearns!!
Its been caught up in a whirlpool of hate, brought on
by childhood misfortunes & pain…
Unable to surface & bring out to the open, because
my heart's been locked with dread & heavy a chain…
I constantly stumble in turmoil of why life's plan for
me is so wickedly cold…there's never any answer that
really makes any sense, just a "true" brother's medicine
& spirit I embrace & hold…I come for this like a
moth to a flame, a powerful magnet my soul is pulling
for…It's just one of my burning untold stories of bur-
ied pain, behind another closed door…
I've never really looked for that perfect excuse of how
this came to be…Only because now that it's up to me
to be as strong as a 100-year old oak tree…to look
up and see the eyes of "true" men, this is what I came
for…That's where "my" key that unlocks the emo-
tional roller coaster behind my hidden door…But, it's
only just one of many paths I have to journey and
make…Among a circle of warriors with medicine &
empathy that's truly not fake…I've searched for ten
years in this hellish maze of cement walls, for just one
true man…I came up empty handed time & time
again except in this very circle - I surely can…So for
this I am truly grateful and continue to look forward
to each & every day…For once in my life my spirit is
free, among a group of good men I can proudly say!!

~ Puma Who Matters ~

Untitled Number Nine

Inner depth, inner strength, inner selves,
inner hell, inner turmoil, inner Circle.
Around a blazing fire Warriors are thrown
into the eyes of childhood.
Screeching and writhing with pain
their bodies tense
as their Warrior souls travel to the distant past
to heal the broken child.
Medicine men sit still with wounded eyes
and their skin is blackened by 3rd degree burns.
The fire still roars and miraculously the scabs
slowly peels to reveal new eyelids.
Visions of men born from the foresight of one man
to instill an everlasting bond
from Warriors from different tribes,
murderers and thieves.
We are now holy men on holy ground
brothers with the same goal.
To travel towards an inner depth
seeking ones inner strength
to heal our inner selves
Inner turmoil
finally becoming one Inner Circle.

~ Dancing Cobra ~

I Too Am Wounded

❧

I see the wounds.
So many wounds inflicted on so many innocent young kids.
I know you're one of them,
and I'm one of them,
and damn near every man alive is one of them.
We have all been wounded
and it's not right, it's flat out wrong.
And still every day it goes on, wounds are inflicted,
and you and I are tossed into a fucked up world,
and told: "learn to live with it."
Well damn it, I'm learning to.
And every time I look at one of my wounds,
I want to scream: who did this to me and why?
And now that I'm looking at these wounds
what can I hope to find
hidden in the deep dark depths of my past?
And what am I suppose to do with it when I do find it?
I'm still not real sure,
and yet still I keep looking.
And I'm getting pretty good at finding these wounds.
I'm learning how these wounds work against me, how they hurt me in
ways I never understood before.
I'm finding when I know this
I can better defend myself.
My wounds need to be treated,
that's what the Circle does,
that's what my brothers do.
I too am wounded.

~ *Painted King* ~

The Eyes on the Water

It is the unexpected smile
that frightens me the most.
It's silent touch of love
that aching feeling in my belly
always so eager to re-connect.
I claim to hate
ignorance
and yet,
I shower in the currents of her waterfall.
I lust for love and adventure
but I can't seem
to get past
my own dimension.
I am looking for a soul
in mirrors of dirty water.
I'm drowning in despair
and talking-to the eyes looking back;
"It is not their fault" they say.
Nature intended us to be
this way…
I saw myself
and ran.

~ *Fierce Fox* ~

Coma

∾

In a coma yet still alive.
I have felt the flames of hell scorch my flesh.
I played with demons with no regard for life.
I have bit back screams
as bullets were dug out of my body,
I've felt the steel blade cut through my skin
and I only smiled a sadistic smile.
I watched my brother die in the street
I seen his eyes glaze over,
I heard his last words,
"well shit"
and then all that was left was the shell of a broken biker
and a pool of blood in the street.
And still I wore my scars like badges of honor,
my scars and tattoos were medals
of some perverted war I was raging against myself.
I don't recall now what I was warring against
or even what I hoped to win.
Now I sit in this cell with years and years to think,
I realize it's as if I am in a coma yet still alive.
Like a coma I didn't have to feel
I was emotionally dead inside.
I didn't have to feel I just had to stay alive.

~ Painted King ~

Window

*

I'm stuck in the middle.
I can't change or be apart of any of it.
I watch both sides.
I see the "man's" hidden tears stream down his tattooed face.
I see the warm California rain wash away
the trash and bring life anew.
I see the man search his books and his inner soul,
seeking some kind of validation for hope.
I watch the deer and the turkeys romp and play,
enjoying life as it is today.
I watch and on both sides of me,
it's need
that dictates the view I see.
On one side it's a need to grow.
And on the other side
it's just a need to be.
I'm stuck in the middle,
I'm the prison cell window
who sees it all.

~ Painted King ~

Walk Wrong

I walk wrong, I talk wrong, I play wrong and I act wrong.
Hardass, first class, biker, gang member, killer, liar, thief,
Cheat, convict, blood bathing bastard,
Scarred, marred real tough guy.
It blows my mind that all that pure crap
Is what I tend to talk about.
I'm real quick to remind any one and, everyone,
How many S.H.U. terms I've done.
How many stabbings I got under my belt.
How many race riots I have been in.
How many club wars I fought.
I talk of crimes and killing
Like they are highlights in my sorry ass life.
This was mentioned to me the other day and it fucked me up,
How can this be true?
I'm so much more in tune with myself, to talk or act this way.
I started to argue the fact when it hit me,
I do that, I do that all the fucking time.

Me who hates guys who do that, does it as much as anyone.
So now I want to know what's that about?
What's under that?
Do I play tough so no one will ever know I'm scared?
Do I try to sell myself so I will be liked?
So no one will know how alone I feel?
I got to get a grip on this.
I know who I am and I know who it is I want to be.
I know what I've done and I know what I want to do.
I need to teach myself how to walk right.
And I need to teach myself how to talk right,
I need to teach myself how to play right,
And how to act right.
I need to embrace who I long to be,
Not who I have been…

~ Painted King ~

You Are My Brother

∽

You are my Brother, I know your heart and you know mine.
I know your sadness and you know mine. I have seen your
Dreams and you have seen mine.
I have shared your joy and you have shared mine.
I have seen you transformed and you have seen me
Transformed. I do not judge you and you do not judge me.
You are my brother not for who you have been or who you
May someday become, but for who you are right now.
You are my brother who is loved and understood. You were made my
brother by your truth and compassion, you are my brother
Forged from years of pain, sorrow and sadness.
Years of being alone made you my brother, and it made you
Understand the worth of being loved.
Never forget you are my brother...

~ *Painted King* ~

Our Journey, the Last Blow Has Been Made Now I Wait

Death has risen his mighty hand against me, and with the final stroke of
his blade has cut the thread of life from my liver.
But it is nothing new.
I am neither special, nor condemned!
The hand that seals my fate is the same hand and will be lifted against
every human that crosses the face of mother earth.
From the ancient one's who were the first to leave footprints in the mud,
to the one's of the future who will leave footprints in the clouds.
It is all the same, there is no difference, you and me, them and us…
Our paths are intertwined, woven one inside the other. The journey we
are on is the same, the journey of life and the journey of death.
But as I sit here in this sacred place with you, and read the words I have
scratched out of my broken soul, upon my death, I ask you my brothers,
to tell my mother and father, that I no longer trespass against others!
That I no longer strike out in anger!
That I no longer hate because I do not understand!
That I no longer blame others from my shortcomings!
That I am no longer a mean ugly despicable human being!
Upon my death, I ask you my brothers, to tell my mother and father,
that I held out a trembling hand to help another man.
That I reached into my soul to reclaim my true nature.
That I washed my face in tears of love for my daughter.
That I have tried to give back what I have taken.
That I am a kinder and gentler man in my death, than I was in life.
I want them to see and to know who I really am, how far I have come,
the things I've seen, the lessons I've learned, the tears I've cried.
The Journey I'm On.

~ Indio ~

Last Sunday

Men, wild souls, friends of mine. We crawl out from under rocks, out of the tops of trees, pull ourselves from muddy rivers, We stumble from back alley bars, ghettos, trailer parks and reservations. From big city neighborhoods, and old country towns, barrios, housing projects and out of cardboard boxes. But we're all the same here. Wearing blue. Trapped in stone. Alone. We come here to our sanctuary within our prison, as men with an idea. Sharing perception and peacefully accepting confrontation.

Seeking illumination, and sometimes even witnessing, the "conception" of our own redemption. Am I going to come to our Inside Circle, and with one hand wipe the tears from my brothers face? And with my other hand, beat my ideas into his body? Somehow trying to validate to myself that I'm right and he's wrong? Isn't it a special gift that I've been given, that I have a place I can come & cry or laugh if I need to? And am I going to do everything I can to help & listen to the man next to or across from me? Or am I only interested when it's about me?

Am I going to come here and represent this madhouse & the insanity?

Or am I going to come here & represent my compassion & humanity?

Am I going to let down myself & my friends from the streets? The same ones who's dreams are about helping me? Who have treated me better than I've been treated in over a decade? With respect, love and dignity?

Wouldn't the administration love to say, I told you so.
It's a waste of time trying to help those souls.
Am I going to prove them right?
Or am I going to show them that they're wrong?
Have my fingertips become so numb, that I no longer
know how to feel?
Or is the only way I know I'm alive, is when I'm
hurting myself & others?
What I seen here last Sunday, scared the hell out of
me.
Not for the fear of physical wounds, but for the
wounds that were almost
inflicted upon our ability to change & grow.
For how much each one of us has to lose, and how
close we came.
I know & believe that you, myself, everyone in our
Circle is a far better
human being than society would like you to believe.
But we all have to believe and faith in each other.

~ Indio ~

Choking

❧

Has anybody got a glass of water? I seem to be chok-
ing here.
I was choking the day I seen my Grandpa David slap-
ping his daughter Robin in the hallway that day. I was
too little and too scared to say anything. But I seen it
and it made me choke. I was choking the day I found
out he died, I never had the courage to ask him why
and now he's gone, and I loved him. I was choking
the day my mother and father split up, and I thought
everything was okay before that. I was confused and
didn't understand what was going wrong. I guess they
thought I didn't need to know, because they never told
me. I was choking the day my mother moved that
other man in the house. My sisters were too young
to understand, but I knew what he was there for. It
made me sick with anger.
Can somebody please help me here? Can't you see
I'm choking? I was choking the day I dropped out of
school in the 10th grade and no one ever asked me to
go back. I deserved that much. I was choking the day
I realized I should have been smart enough to look
out for myself and stayed in school in the first place. I
was choking the day I came back from up north and
I called my best friend, Kelly Shehane's house, his
mother Linda answered and I asked if I could speak
to Kelly? She asked if this was some kind of sick

joke? And when she realized it was me, she broke out in sobbing tears and said he went into his bedroom two weeks ago and blew his brains out. What! Are you going to let me choke to death? Can you please slap me on the back! I was choking that first day I stuck a needle in my arm at fourteen and it was a good friend of mine who handed it to me. I was choking the day I came back from work and Jackie had packed up everything including our daughter, Trisha, and ran off to Kansas someplace with some guy named Tony. That was twelve years ago and I haven't seen them since. I was choking the day I came to prison and I'm still choking. I'm choking for the missed opportunities. I'm choking for the loss of humanity. I'm choking for the tears I have cried.
I'm choking for the letters that never came.
I'm choking because I hate.
I'm choking because I love.
I'm choking because I'm scared.
I'm choking because my cry for help was never heard.
Has anybody got a glass of water?

~ *Indio* ~

Silent Echoes

I sat there confused, drugged and helpless.
Feeling the effects of this self imposed disease.
How can I fight this demon
when it has rooted itself in every fiber of my body;
it has broken down all my walls
it has left me out in the open
it has crippled me with shame.
I'm terrified that there won't be any mystical cure.
This is just too much to bear.
It's poison is so infectious it has blocked any way out.
I'm going mad!
I need to take the dive, it has to be now…
Nothing, just silence, dead silence stinking the air,
clouding my vision slapping me awake.
But why?
All this time it was me…
That beast—that painful enigma, it's all mine.
I was the one keeping it alive.
It wasn't any foreign element.
There weren't any echoes or shadows plotting.
No roaming conspiracies
just another battle
against insanity.
All inside my own head
buried deep in my own brain.
All that time spent
in futile quest, only to find
it was just silence—
the vivid stench of silence.

~ *Fierce Fox* ~

In Here

❧

Every man has a history
Every man is a story
A child, a son
Some are fathers
others are brothers, simply man…
bound by the same language;
–Compassion–
reaching each other
It may, or may not make sense but, it is what we have
what we feel what has been clouded,
buried deep under all those
shells of rules, colors, and patterns.
We speak to each other without the concerns
of this here and now…
We forget our colors, our rules and connect,
as if we were all from the same household…
Forgetting for a few moments
all the legends, all the bad blood…
Imposed by ignorance, by what we call: the system.
Let me tell you my brother my heart aches
my choices are limited
but see me, not as your rival.
See yourself, a white man, a black man, a brown man,
a son, a father, a brother,
a fellow human a man with many faults
a man in need a man in search of meaning
–Simply a Man–
Don't make unfounded judgments
learn this beautiful language
with no boundaries…
feel for a moment what it is to be you.

~ *Fierce Fox* ~

My Brother

❦

Desperado, Outcast, Outlaw, Renegade, Scoundrel, Murderer, Robber,
Thief, Con-Man, Junky, Alcoholic, Dope-Fiend, Abuser, Prisoner.

If you can see your face in any of these words
You are my brother.

Hated, Despised, Untrusted, Misunderstood, Degraded, Humiliated,
Suppressed, Exiled, Shunned, Unwanted, Thrown-Away, Lost, Dying,
Dead, Lonely, Homeless, Poor, Tragedy, Misery, Sick, Diseased, Broken,
Prisoner!

If you can see your face in any of these words,
You are my brother!

Seeking, Teaching, Learning, Growing, Hoping, Changing,
Understanding, Loving, Sharing, Helping, Wanting, Touching, Accepting,
Tolerating, Praying,
Prisoner!

If you can see your face in any of these words,
You are my brother!

Black, White, Yellow, Brown, Red, Catholic, Protestant, Jehovah, Baptist,
Muslim, Native American
Paganist, Atheist, Prisoner!

If you can see your face in any of these words,
You are my brother!

Because I am all of these things and much more
I am human.

~ Indio ~

Untitled

᷈

For a few brief moments
I touched the sacred.
With laughing tears
I felt released.
All my life I've misinterpreted
the language of emotions
and proud I was of my
foolish misunderstandings
while aggressively defending
my stupidity. I thoughtlessly
crushed all else but my own.
I move a little more carefully now
and I want to touch
the sacred again.
Maybe a little longer next time?

~ Healing Wolf ~

Untitled Number Eight

❧

Like a angel who has fallen from the sublime heavens
I've been exposed to what life is all about.
I reminisce of how I use to be:
lazy, empty of true feelings.
I've trembled with my silent screaming.

Why must I expose my empty childhood
for all to see
just to change my silent soul?
My subtle ambition to change is lost to the naked eye.

Sublime images of being free
fill my empty soul
to the point of agony.
I've trembled from screaming at my silent heart

Sublime images of being truly free
fill my empty silent heart;
I've trembled with pain at the loss of my innocence
screaming at ghosts only I can see.

~ Loving Leopard ~

Untitled Number One

❧

I'd rather die

than give you control

once more

I can't take this shit much longer

Good Bye to you

and your point of view

I see clearly now

your thoughts of who I should be

doesn't matter once and for all

I think for myself

you can run

you can't hide

from the truth

You're as fucked as me.

~ Loving Leopard ~

The Death Song of My Joy

❧

When acceptance is based on approval,

Disapproval means they'll leave, they're gone.

Affection & acceptance is in degrees.

Rejecting ultimatums disguised as requests,

Recognition comes too late, they're gone.

When I'm uninteresting they're not interested.

Damn it. I've sung these songs too,

Stealing other peoples joy all my life.

~ Healing Wolf ~

After All My Work

❧

What helped me get past and through my fear,

was the I don't give-a-fuck attitudes.

I needed the power of my many angers,

to face my many fears.

I've cussed, raged and exploded out of chairs,

the Circle is skilled at raging space.

Now I stalk my fears,

they are guides to my medicine.

My body talks to me through fear,

the complicated language of self love.

~ Healing Wolf ~

To Do

They told me what I did,

They tell me what to do,

They tell me what not to do,

What I need to do,

What's best for me to do.

So I judge them for not doing what they say

they're going to do.

I found my path under unbearable truths.

What to do with old, old wounds,

And new ways of healing.

Clarity to decide what to do,

not blindly groping in the dark,

falling off the path.

~ Healing Wolf ~

Greatness

⟋

In my mind, I always had this powerful desire, hope and faith that greatness was possible for me.

That I would find great men who would welcome me into their presence after I proved myself worthy of greatness.

In my life time, I'm realizing this is a childish part of my hero's journey, a fairy tale.

The truth is, what I'm experiencing, is that I must push myself beyond my ordinary limits into my power, my depth, my integrity and authenticity.

I've discovered, we're all equipped to be great, all the magnificence of greatness resides in each and every one of us.

Greatness now surrounds me in different aspects and forms of it's mysterious growth.

Day after week after month after year, I watch men being great and others serving that greatness.

None of'em aware of how really great they are during the intensity of their agonizing struggles.

Now I see greatness is not a rare quality of a few men.

Now I see that every man can learn how to be more great for longer periods of time, more often, in more necessity.

Now I know what it means when a dream comes true, that a fairy tale matures into a great reality.

~ Healing Wolf ~

A Years Reflection

❧

I went to love,
but was loved everyday.
I went to educate,
but learned more than I ever knew.
I went to listen,
but was heard for the first time.
I went to patch wounds,
but left restored.
I entered ignorant,
but developed wisdom.
I entered fearful,
but gained courage.
I entered blind,
but began to see.
I entered hopeful,
but departed confident.
What happened I can't explain,
for truth is never revealed through words.

~ Truth Seeker ~

In the Words of Creed

*

With arms wide open
Where healing is sought
From pains given, pains brought.
Then there's trust and hope
And the doors, the doors;
When the doors open to the gauntlet of suspicion,
With open arms and hearts of pain,
Affliction and feelings begin to pour
To pour in ciphers, carpets and rugs,
From the scorned hearts of thugs, the hardest of men.
Free and enslaved to drugs, men of all persuasion gathered
For the sacred occasion, the shedding of skins
The skins of betrayal colored by hate
That has cultivated a mans danger
Now opposed, by willingness to work, the courage
To search with truth exposing shame
To a place where there is self empowerment & medicine
To be gained.
Unforgetting that there's some one who needs me,
Who share the pain & knows the pain
And what it's like being insane.
Someone who needs me in those hurting drops of blood
Drips of sweat & drenches of tears,
The fears once unknown now are shown to someone
Who really cares…

~ Conquering Tiger with Divine Compassion ~

What I See in the World Is Me

~

The love I see in the world is me.
The hate I see in the world is me.
I am what I love in the world.
I am what I hate in the world.
Not what loves me in the world.
Not what hates me in the world.
I am what I love and hate
and I have the power in this moment
to choose.
I won't wait until the death bed to do my choosing
or until I believe I have earned it,
that day never comes.
I have had the power to choose all along.
The world loving me or hating me
is on them – they choose too.
I am what I hate in this world,
not what hates me.
I am what I love in this world,
not what loves me.
And the truth hidden on the other side of this coin
is there is no real choice – that too is illusion,
there is only understanding what I truly am.

~ Lion That Sometimes Catches Fire ~

I'm Not Longer Alone

Alone no longer

Hope for better understanding

I my new drug

One that will keep me high

For the rest of my life

I have opened up myself to myself

I dissect my past

To unleash my future

I have taken off my mask

That I've worn for my whole life

I can see things clearly now

I'm not as fucked as I thought I was

~ Loving Leopard ~

Untitled Number Fifteen

✍

I've been living a lie for way too long

All this shit about not being a man if you cry

I've fallen to my knees plenty of times

Screaming at the heavens above

Asking God why?

I've read in the Good Book

That God only gives what you can handle

The flames inside

Is dimming, flickering

Wanting to give up it's fight

To guide my way

I've rebuilt the walls around my heart

You so easily tore down

Feeling exposed

Like a fish out of water

I can't breathe

~ Loving Leopard ~

Mine

❧

Through my words of poetry
I've found my need to live
Is stronger than my will to die
What a tangle web of deceit
I've believed in
The emotions I feel
Remind me of a mountain
I've struggled to climb
Never reaching the top
Knowing the peak is within my reach
I'm shedding my old armor
I want to feel shiny and new
Looking back on my old life's lies
I've realized the truth
It wasn't you who was fucked
It was me
Only feeling what I thought you wanted me to
I'm growing up now
My past is my past
My future is my future
Today is mine

~ Loving Leopard ~

Didn't Know

~

You're a poet to capture lives,
Hearts and carves your words
upon worthy frames
When didn't know
Convincing are fairy tale stories,
and certain theories that always
collide in the right of time
Envisage fiction notions
While emotions trivialize vicious
Desperate, psychotic
Schemes to hunt hearts
While I beat ravenous, and anxious
Believing the enormous protocol
Defeats I'll conquer with no respect
But will sparkle carving my name
Unto well deserve minds and hearts on frames
Gambling to a present,
Gambling to a future the worthiest
Of attitude it is to conquer
What would keep us from falling victim?
Fears of death alone!
gambling for my life or death
Quick steps I give to be the best.
I can no longer sustain loses
I can no longer be victim
To the oppressive,
I can no longer evade
Finding the worth within.
I can no longer stay stuck
With noting good to gain,
Within alone I am who I am
On of all on paper and pen.

~ *Significant Elk Who Soars* ~

Another Day Away From Reality
❧

Days just seem to vanish
Night comes without a hope.
Television shows me the latest news...
Five were killed, no guns involved;
No, it wasn't a crime of passion
Not even a deranged gang-banger
Looking for a cheap thrill they say it was mom
But how O God why?
She had a deep depression
Medication didn't cure it
Five were killed
Nothing can be done.
Now I think of why,
Of my own life
Trying to find answers
For my troubled soul.
Maybe, we all got it, this demon
Driving us to insanity
Some stronger than others
To keep it engaged.
I shed a tear thinking of them
Those five small faces wild with fear.
They say the mind did it
It wasn't entirely her fault
-She was insane-
Now she must be put on trial
Her own life is on the line.
I wonder, if she hears their cries,
Or if she sees their faces begging her to stop.
There were five mom took them all
Maybe it was written all this way,
Maybe it was after all, our human's way.

~ Fierce Fox ~

Memories & Possibilities

❧

Looking past faded memories of a life lived too fast
Discarding futuristic glances at hopes
Of tomorrow's possibilities.

Yesterdays are only what once was,
And hold no power today.
Tomorrow's are only dreams
That may or may not
Some day become real.

But today, right now.
This is real this is
What I got.

This is not faded memories
Nor is it mere hopes
Or unfounded possibilities.

This is life.
I feel my heart beating,
Blood flowing
This is what's real.

And if I dare to release my grip on
Yesterdays and tomorrow's.

I can feel spirit right now
And that sure is not no
Memories or possibilities
It's fact.

~ Painted King ~

April – Month Four

RISKS, TRUTH, REGRET, FED-UP, SECRETS, ANGER

There are inherent dangers in taking risks and not taking risks by speaking truths, secrets regrets etc. The danger is in the constant and growing aggravation until one is fed-up and the resulting reactions, which often leads to anger.

The time that is past for unsaid words with unintended results. Nothing saves us from fear but ourselves, often we've mated with the beast of fear.

Pretending not to care until everyone believes it, then no-one else does. Who invites us to see the real them, the fierce, violent feral part that can get backed into corners of playing by the rules? The danger is of speaking the truth and there are many who avoid it. Some get fed-up and trapped, but then they're stuck doing it and forced to live with the pain.

In the pursuit of healing, is there a breaking point, that could leave us to wallow in our pain? Sometimes one desire tops all others: drugs, incomplete feelings or hiding behind smiles.

Blinded by hate, weighted with negativity, emotional vomit, wounded eyes, unfathomable regrets, impotent but longing for the power to fight them. Misshapen and deformed shadows all are welcomed by the Clowns of Compassion who serve the sacred Circles in curing the plague of shadows.

Simplicity

❧

A pillar of truth stands unknowingly simple in design.

Hand carved by the hands of a simpleton.

Happily satisfied with the meager wages being paid.

He is ignorant of deceit and lies.

He just chips and carves,

lost within the complexities of his trade.

He knows not of the condescending tone he is spoken upon

he just smiles.

In his completion,

he stands knowingly of his own perfection.

~ Dancing Cobra ~

A Cold Wind Blows

ॶ

A cold wind blows across this land,
a twisting, tangled mess, of dusty weeds and severed hands.
Of white picket fences and goodbye smiles,
of never to be love affairs, an unborn child.
A cold wind blows across this land.
Like the flatulence that comes from an impish, vicious
little twit of a man.
George W. Bush or Saddam Hussein,
each one an anomaly to their cause.
Each one insane, each to blame for their pain.
Dressed up nice, festooned in the decorative chains of hate,
shined up boots, belly's full from the lies they ate.
But when lightning strikes,
and the conquering scourge of war has brought its fright,
when compassion is dead and the whole world is forced to fight.
When the calamity and desolation of the battle has come
and weapon's thunder, while faceless army's plunder
and all is asunder.
These two dogs will be lying safely, under shameful covers.
A cold wind blows across this land,
but the price of 25¢ I'll sell you a prayer,
says the good "ole" preacher man.
Guaranteed to get you all the way to the promised land.
So with a feathered tongue, and a golden wing,
for just the price of a quarter,
through the gates of heaven I will sing.
"A cold wind blows across this land."

~ *Indio* ~

A Man's Fear

&

A man's fear lives in the center of his existence.
It sharpens and crushes his emotions. It shelters him from his enemies.
It trashes and destroys his joy. Powerful as it is
a man's fear doesn't let him live in peaceful awakening.
All the talk, all the writing won't save a man from his own fear.
This fear has become the very source of life
only a man himself can cast away this monster out of his house
it doesn't matter how much, it is said
or the endless time spent in prayer
the fear of a man is stubborn and instinctive as the lion's fury
it fills him with doubt it mocks his pretentious sense of stability
I am a man!
I know what I'm talking "about" I've mated with this beast
it has now become the host and I, a guest to its domains...
painful mourning
morning shouts
child's sorrows
madness of the mind
anguish of the soul
it encompasses all
it is alive and capriciously ahead of each step a man takes
fooling, and tearing him apart
manifesting his weakness
anytime it feels threaten
a man's fear is so rigidly rooted
in his spine that it has no origin
nor an end
it is undone, baseless, concrete
it breathes life but kills him inside
a man's fear dwells in his mind.

~ *Fierce Fox* ~

Loss of My Soul

The loss of my soul never was my goal
in a dark and lonely place,
I reach for emotion but find not even a trace.
I feel my heart beating in my chest,
so what happened to my compassion, understanding and all the rest?
At one time I was a man who had enough feelings to freely give.
Now I seem to only be a shell that somehow continues to live.
I look into the sky
and search for a feeling of peace, comfort or joy.
When was it that all my tenderness was thrown away,
like a child's broken toy?
I possess an active brain
the same blood still flows through my veins.
And I still long for a gentle caress,
its absence brings such burning pains.
I know where I am and I know what I have done
I forfeited freedom and I let down my wife and son.
I still possess one emotion;
it's a growing fear that I will end up
an un-caring zombie like so many others in here.
The loss of my soul never was my goal...

~ Painted King ~

Un-Said Words

~

Thoughts never shared,
dreams never to come true
and words that will forever go un-said.
All tangled together in my head.
Feelings that can never be put into words,
and if they were who would hear them?
When I who feel them can't even understand them.
When laying in the dark trying to sleep
but sleep won't come,
the thoughts,
dreams and un-said words making my brain numb.
When I close my eyes
and look deep into the forgotten places of my soul
I see my thoughts,
my dreams and all them un-said words that have no faces.
So much to say and no way to say it.
So many words that need to be said
but will they mean the same thing once they are said?

~ *Painted King* ~

The Kids Always Pay

*

When I allow myself to close my eyes and dwell on the destruction
I have left in my wake, I am overcome with shame.

There were so many times I could have fed a hungry child or
helped a battered woman. But, there was not any profit in that so I
turned my back and ignored it.

When it started to get to me, I would just ride faster and shoot
quicker. Oh what a monster I was.

Run and hide but do not dare look inside.
I always kept my eyes wide open, all the better to watch my
back. Still I was blind.

Collecting debts that dope fiends made. Now when I look back I
see that it was the poor kids that had to.

~ Painted King ~

If I Was Stronger

~

Lost in a mist that hides all I know,
living in a world that dictates just what I can show.
Feelings are hid so deep inside me
I can almost forget that they are even there.
But that ain't me,
it ain't who I want to be.
I want to care
I want to open up and share;
I wish I could say how I feel,
I wish I could scream or cry when I hurt,
just throw my head back and howl
and let it all out,
that would be frowned on without a doubt.
So I play my role,
I walk the walk I talk the talk
I fight like a possessed demon when I have to.
But it's all fake, it's all a lie
it's just what I have to do.
Maybe if I was stronger I would refuse to live this lie anymore,
I would just wash the blood off my hands,
learn how to be a strong person.

~ Painted King ~

Little Boy Blue

❧

Little boy in the window
Won't let you come out and play
Mama says that she loves you
She don't love you today
Little scars on your body
Little scars on your mind
Little secrets you're keepin'
Get bigger every time.

Ooo, what you gonna do?
Ooo, little boy blue

Tonight you stay at the neighbors
You know just what that means
They know you don't like it
No point in makin' a scene
Now them hands on your body
Can't hear you when you cry
If you try to tell mama
Mama says it's a lie.

Ooo, what you gonna do?
Ooo, little boy blue.

~ Shaman's Key ~

Cancer

❧

I'm seething this fucking nightmare.
I'm living and this reality strikes dead center, weary of the
tireless banter, it's eating me up like cancer, maybe it's
fuckin' brain tumor, note my humor, I might laugh and smile
but I've been rotting inside for awhile.
Can't really remember if I was ever that soft spoken child.
I'm restless; anticipation continually building.
Can't really see what I'm feeling.
It's probably a monster who can't stand to be trapped any
longer.
It's getting even stronger and believe me I've tried to kill it
in honor of my father.
Scream and holler, they'll be no rescue for you, choking me
till
I'm black and blue.
I hate this shit, this fuckin' life I'm in, I hate this fuckin'
world.
God please release me from my sin.

~ Dancing Cobra ~

I Don't Get It???

~

Why do birds sing…So pretty…

in a world where,

children are treated so badly, everyday?

Why are flowers…So beautiful….

when, bombs, bullets & madness…

permeate the air…?

Why does anyone want a president….

that has the record for the most…executions….

or one that only lies…when…his…lips move…?

Why can't people communicate…without using cuss words…?

Why don't more people…or all people care about the truth…?

Why do people…spend…money…on…tobacco…so.

they can…poison…their self…and others?

I don't get it…

~ Unknown ~

Unknown

～

Teeth snap closed to grief
too choked by terror
of these deep chested,
guttural emotions that
will devour me whole
if I suddenly let go.

It is all here, friend – the HIV patient
Scratching like a junky jonesing
for a fix – body bags and toe tags –
and they drop like flies, two
and three a week…
Give me a poem that decries life's
tragedies
so I can appreciate life's inviolable
sanctity.

Not only to survive, but to live
and flourish with creativity,
becoming a flame for further
combustions, like mine.

~ Patrick Nolan ~

Breaking Point

Where's your breaking point?
Can I really bring every truth?
Are all my doubts welcome here?
I carry suspicion everywhere,
I wear it like a shirt.
Is it welcome here too?
Will I push you to your limit,
if I confront you about contradictions
in your speech and actions?

Where's your breaking point?
Will you forgive me if I doubt you in the circle?
Really?
You won't hold a grudge?
You won't nurture silent resentments
when I request a Warrior Round?

Where's your breaking point?
In seeking my truths
am I pushing you beyond your breaking point?
If you leave the circle because I push too hard,
where will that leave my community?

Where's your breaking point?

~ Healing Wolf ~

Every Dog Has It's Day

Take a puppy and put him on a chain, kick him beat
him become the source of all his pain. mistreat him
day and night. laugh as the puppy tries to bite.

Now the joke is up its not funny anymore. The puppy
broke his chain and he is coming through the door.

You can run but you can't hide. For years the puppy's
rage quietly grew inside.

Now you're left to face him all alone. As the puppy
rips the flesh from the bone, as you scream and go
insane, it dawns on you, that now the puppy is the
source of all your pain.
So it seems there is truth in what they say:
Sooner or later every dog has his day...

~ Painted King ~

Carnal

A homeboy was shot the other night
and I was there to see the blood
the pain
the look at death
the feeling of agony.
As I looked at him my blood ran cold.
I felt hatred and need for revenge.
Evil filled my heart,
an explosion grew within.
I tried to hide my deepest thoughts of kicking off a war.
But nothing could relieve my pain of needing to settle the score.
With this in mind
I knelt down and raised my homeboy's head.
At first I thought he had died
But then he looked up and said;
"Hey Carnal I'm going to die behind a foolish game."

~ Unknown ~

Untitled Number Three

❧

Me and my fishing poles were dear friends.

My wife found them everywhere,

shoes, coat pockets, socks,

stuffed in porno mags.

I was a classic fiend,

caring more about my harpoons

than my own health, dreams and love.

Scrapping together change and things to sell,

for another ride to blissful hell.

Sweating, clammy, bones aching.

I've got to find out who has the best bait.

It's fishing time.

~ Loving Leopard ~

Untitled Number Twelve

Someone please miss me

I'm still here

I still feel emotions

I bleed just like you

I'm dying on the inside

as I sit here smiling at you

my wounds won't ever heal

like scar tissue

memories of her to always remind me

of what I loved and lost

do you want me to open up

I'm scared too

I have no idea

what will spin forth

so I hold it in

one day I will explode.

~ Loving Leopard ~

Untitled

❧

The discretion infused with demoralization crowds me into isolation. Spawn of glen, will I ever live again? How can I fend for myself in this maggot-infested pool of worthless men? It has no end. Afterbirth, thrown to the side. Homies come to pick me up in a "G" ride. How do I live? I don't fit in. My mother conceived me into sin. Intoxicated by feelings, I spin. Surrounded by scavengers, snakes and scabies. Waging war within. Oh, when will my freedom begin? I want to go home, but I can't find the door. I could care less if you were a horror! Lock me up and throw away the key. Why can't anyone see me?

Do I have a right? Do I have a dream? Do I have a care? Can my voice be seen? Drowning in a swamp that's pulling me under, I look to my right and left, plunder, pillage, rob and steal, and kill - take all you can! That my son will make you a man! Twisted, misconstrued and damned, those around me, I really can't understand! Outwardly stretched, raised to the sky, the hands of many willing to die. Clouded confusion, constrains and confines, consistent with imploding my mind.

Flush him! Flush him! One…Two…Three! No… No…No, we'll get married, you and me! A beating saved my life? How can this be? She wouldn't listen. I slapped her once, you see! Is it true Michaelea, what you say? I was left to hold that bag, condemned to pay, each and everyday, for all his play? Is that a crock of shit or what! How can my life make a difference, and for what? How can I tell what's going on outside my hell? It's ok, it's not that bad, I really do miss my dad. I wish I could hug him and say good-bye. But all I have left is a tear in my eye. It eats and consumes me, until I long to die. I can't feel the pain. Yet I know every cell is saturated all the way through to the membrane. They drive me insane, the "what ifs" and "if onlys." All I ever do is feel lonely. Want you to come hold me. I know God makes, shapes, and molds me. Yet, this too is foreign to me, surrounded by strangers. When is my life not in danger! What's familiar, what's unknown, it's all blurred in this desert I'll never call home.

~ Loving Leopard ~

Claribel Alegria

℘

My black cat doesn't know

he will die one day

he doesn't cling to life

as I do

he leaps from the roof top

light as air

climbs the tamarind tree

barely scratching it

doesn't dread crossing bridges

or dark alley ways

nor the perfidious scorpion

my black cat falls in love

with every cat he meets

he refuses to be snared

by a single love

the way I did.

~ *Loving Leopard* ~

My Experience With Truth

~

Once I spoke a truth and a wise old warrior reasoned it away. I felt like the fool in that song, what a fool believes, a wise man can reason away.

My experience with truth is that it is unwanted, painful, gets attacked, ignored, laughed at and reasoned away.

Speaking truths have caused friendships to end, fights, arguments, stabbings, shootings, riots, I've witnessed these and more.

I believe the wise old warriors can speak truth and disappoint others to be true to themselves.

I'm beginning to wonder if I'm damn near perfect, I haven't been called for a warrior round since I don't remember when.

All the unspoken truths, unspoken for months on end, the unaccountable shadow misbehaviors unlearned about myself.

Years of not being called on the rug, proves what?

If it's not what I do in life that matters, but how I deal with what happens to me that counts, not happening counts.

Maybe I'm just being a damn fool and warrior rounds don't matter after all.

~ Healing Wolf ~

Brain Lock

❧

Sitting in the cell, criticizing the TV, my cellie, and everyone I hear on the tier and in the vent.

But when I'm on the tier, I greet everyone with my phony tier face, acting with no problems.

My guts are in knots with worry, fear, anger and weaknesses I'm not strong enough to express.

Not saying it right, not saying it straight, and secretly glad to hurt the other person.

I embarrassingly disown my shit, blaming everyone else to bully my way out of responsibility.

If not my images will crack and fall off.

Too scared to think straight, pretending everything is alright sitting in brain lock, holding up the image I hate.

~ Healing Wolf ~

Crossing Boundaries

❧

I squirm uncomfortably when someone steps to me

to tell me what I did not ask for.

I resent it, when I'm not asking,

I'm not wanting to hear it.

I want it to be a question, my choice,

not taken without my consent.

If taken, it leaves me with,

unwanted side-effects.

~ Healing Wolf ~

Here

~

I'm not sitting in the circle of sacred space

to suck up all the love and compassion of the warriors,

until they're drained or I'm full.

I'm not here to critically judge,

all work is welcomed and sacred.

I'm here on holy ground to be blessed by Kings,

humbled by Magicians,

strengthened by Warriors and loved by Lovers.

To clarify mysteries, shine on shadows, discover gold,

medicate wounds, tame demons, and step into joy.

The sweetness of hope comforts me through fear,

suspicion, and saying fuck-it, or fuck-you.

Here, the invitation is real.

~ Healing Wolf ~

Seems Obvious

❧

The differences between reading about sex

and having sex

seems obvious.

Wanting her delicious taste in the mouth.

Her feminine musky smell in the nostrils.

The beautiful obscene vision

of her in passionate abandon.

Feeling her hot flesh

rub and pound against you,

and she wraps herself around you,

in the midst of shrieks of joy

and moans of deep satisfaction.

It's the difference

between getting on the rug and talking about it.

Seems obvious.

~ Healing Wolf ~

Hanging Out With Pain

I beat myself down again.

Pain's no friend but we sure hang out often.

He shuts me down into a state of confusion.

I feel lost in a labyrinth that's really a maze,

surrounded by unlocked doors, I won't enter.

If I turn the knob, they'll listen but won't hear me.

Only a dead man from hippo can read my soul.

What do I do? I repress pain.

My mind sucks it up like a black hole.

I prevent any escape because I'm scared.

Scared to look truth in the face.

Scared to accept help.

Scared to reach my potential.

Pain and I hang out another day.

~ Truth Seeker ~

That's Alright

It's getting complicated,
disrupting the peace of people
(frustrated), I'm starting to hate it,
attacks from the negative administration,
on a space that's positive and sacred.
Spirit's work will be done,
(by each and everyone)
so you might as well face it,
(like the sun)
kiss where it don't shine,
I'm gonna keep to my heart
but still expressing my mind
and since I'm speaking truth,
thought I was through with hate,
but I realize I hate your kind
who hate to see struggling men
make the best of their time.
And you can take the candles,
play your games,
but you can't take
the spirit of a man who's
committed to change,
extinguishable flames, got you burning inside
it's your own living hell,
power tripping cause you choose
to despise the power
you can't grasp or see with your
hateful eyes.
And that's alright
And that's alright.

~ Healing Wolf ~

Picking a Dog

~

Are we the brave warriors
Who can express truths with tender compassion
And gentle understanding
That painfully touches the heart
Of the dog in the pound?
The dog in the pound who agreed to listen
To the truth about his abilities
Of medicine and destructive poisons
Without complaining about the fires that these truths ignite?
Can I sit in the sacred dog pound
And hear the uncut, unsanitized bold truths
That describe my brokenness by the warriors of the circle
Speaking the ugly truths that I'm requesting
From all warriors who are able to speak it from their hearts
Inspite of their fear, doubts and regrets?
The brave wounded warriors speaking truths
To the brave wounded dogs in the pound
Who are broken and believe in healing
The poisonous shadows that plague us all
Because there will be no growth or healing
Without understanding and acceptance
Of the holy privilege we share in this gauntlet
In the sacred space we create.

~ *Healing Wolf* ~

Vomit

❧

I wallow in my emotional vomit
Like a pig in his own shit
No matter how I scrub
I smell
I ask people if they smell that stench
They look at me with confusion
In their eyes
So I make excuses
I try to divert their attention
With casual conversation
Sometimes it works
Other times they ask questions
Is everything alright ?
Do you need anything?
I get uncomfortable
My mind is telling me to bolt
My heart just wants an end to this constant pain
Now when I reek with emotional vomit
I know that the smell won't go away
It's all in my head
Do I want to continue to smell it?

~ *Loving Leopard* ~

You Will Never Know

~

You can never know the horror I feel over the pain I
have inflicted on the innocent.
You will never know the demons that dance in my
mind, smashing crashing and destroying the few sane
thoughts that dare sneak past the ever vigilant eye.
You will never know that I scream death screams in my
sleep as I kill the same men over and over every night.
You will never know that I will keep killing these same
men for the rest of my sorry ass life.
You will never know the blood I must sit in when I
close my eyes and look where I have been.
You will never know that I see the dead men
screaming at me when I seek peace.
You will never know that I fight to stay sane when in
the deepest darkest depths of my mind I know I should
have to go crazy for all the pain I have inflicted.
You will never know that no matter what I do,
I will still always be the guy who sat in blood and
laughed at the death I was inflicting.
You will never know that I am scarred that someday I
will crave to sit in the blood again.

~ *Painted King* ~

I Long for the Power to Right Wrongs

❧

I long for the power to right wrongs.
Not just my wrongs but life's wrongs.
The wrongs of a world
that lets a child be born in to
poverty, incest, abuse and neglect.
I long for the power to right wrongs.
I want to right the wrongs of
an innocent runny nose kid
having to learn to live by
brutal rules or die.
I long for the power to right wrongs.
Like the wrong of the little ten year old boy
with a twenty dollar pistol in one pocket
and a handful of rocks in the other.
Just another ghetto statistic.
And it's wrong!
It's wrong when fat overpaid assholes
drive around in $100,000 cars
passing kids digging in the trash trying to find dinner
because they know the only dinner they are going to get
is what they find.
It's wrong but no one cares if they eat.
I long for the power to right wrongs.

~ *Painted King* ~

Wounded Eyes

～

From out of wounded eyes
I am not seen for who I am.
From out of wounded hearts
I am not understood to be a caring man.
Placed upon a thrown
and expected to be more than I am.
And when the standard
surpasses my abilities
wounded eyes fail to see me for who I am.
Wounded hearts inflict cuts to my soul
when they do not see who I am.
A caring man.
So to all of you with wounded eyes and wounded hearts,
let me tell you who I am.
I do not care what color your skin is.
I do not care where you live or have lived.
I do not care if you are rich or poor.
I do not care if you inflict fear or are afraid.
I do care that
your wounded eyes blur your vision
of me.
But let me be real clear.
Because you have decided to judge
me to be something
that does NOT make me that.
It is only what you have decided to see.

~ *Painted King* ~

May - Month Five

MAGIC, MYSTERY, MIRACLES, ILLUMINATION, SACRED, KINGSHIP, BLESSINGS

The emotional pain of living and the perseverance necessary to keep hope alive, is the best energetic space for the mind to open to the clear sight into faith.

The unpredictable timetable of mystical evolution, unknowingly planting the seeds of miracles, the indescribable power of magic. When exploring the depths of one's inner self, rituals can help evoke these experiences. This searching begins in mystery and is often interrupted with foolish impulses. What is supposed to be, and the risks of not being, can be the energy that directs us toward the wilderness within ourselves.

The sensitivities of the dawning of new realities can also drive a man mad and to the limits of the possibilities of divine advice, divine intervention with mystical experiences. Magicians/shamans are the keepers of the way to these dark paths. The secrets of understanding through experiences instead of mental gymnastics. These experiences are like flights from the condemned during this initiation, freed for brief moments from the prison of our bodies, seeing with the heart.

When we look inward, the risks of reaching into the uncomfortable, to communicate with our silent inner witness, are mountains of matter that don't matter, only the truth does.

Sitting in the angst of expecting and finding faith in the end, of hopelessness and the honor of being blessed. Hope is reborn in the faintest ash, the indestructible spirit on the path of initiation. The personal speed of the chase from death to rebirth and, knowing how to be alive with love.

Faith

❧

The One
I sometimes forget
Oh faith, what a beauty you are
Where should I begin to look
Where should I start the quest…
One day
Faced with hopelessness,
I found you.
I was so down
My soul couldn't cope
With the restrains of life.
You made a promise
If only "I"
Should have you,
There are no limits to your grace.
And for this
I give you my soul.

~ Fierce Fox ~

Unknown

❧

On the edge of my seat
the silence falls
I find my place.
Feet rooted to the earth
on the edge of my seat
sitting erect eager waiting
staring at the flame directly ahead. On the edge of my seat
circled up
creating myth
forging my future
healing my past
on the edge of my seat.
Connecting souls
comfortable awake
present.
On the edge of my seat.

~ Silver Wolf that Cares for the Pack ~

The Wizard

❧

Today I watched a wizard with his wand in his hand,
he moved his fingers
and I was instantly struck with the power of his magic.
He caressed his wand with callused fingers,
fingers that have bled,
the blood of passion for magic.
I watched his eyes and I saw the tension
and the madness fade from his face.
I could see the true man come alive
as his fingers danced across the wand,
Man, Marty is one hell-of-a Wizard…
I feel his magic every time I see his guitar in his hand.

~ Painted King ~

Gang Member

❧

I'm a gang member.
I'm a member of toughest gang in the world.
when my gang gets together in one place,
the power is a force that can't be beat.
My gang has killers, robbers, and thieves,
guys who have lived with hate, anger and blood most of their lives.
My gang is hard as rock, strong as steel.
My gang is the Inside Circle.
We're a bunch of men who know how to be real.
We know how to cry without having to wipe the tears away,
so no-one will see them.
We know how to be afraid and talk about our fears.
We know how to take hold of our shame
and look at what it means to us.
My gang is men brave enough to care about their brothers,
in a place where caring is often mistook for weakness.
My gang is men with enough foresight
to see past the cement and the razor wire.
My gang can see and speak the truth,
that they want more than prison wants them to have.
My gang wants to be alive not just breathe,
but to really be alive, to love, to laugh, to cry,
to grab a-hold of a brother and know he is loved,
and that he know how to love.
So I say with pride in my heart,
I'm a gang member.
I'm a member of the Inside Circle…

~ *Painted King* ~

Unknown

☙

If I close my eyes
and look to what will come,
I have to smile.
If I close my eyes
and look to where I have been,
I have to cry.
And if I can force myself
to look at where I am today
right now
then I find myself smiling
through the tears of joy
That I'm finally
growing up.
My mind is open,
my sight is clear;
I know I won't destroy myself
while I'm here.

~ Loving Leopard ~

Untitled Number Seven

My Silent witness who never sleeps says:
"I will wait on you for eternity,
On all you know to do and yet to know.
We will walk this path together."

The tears you withhold I see.
Underneath your anger, I feel your fear.
The saltiness of the unshed tear,
Burns emotions unexpressed.

I can taste your shame,
Feel the gloom of your sorrow,
And the power of your urges,
All you withhold for your puffed up ego.

The child in your heart is caged,
Terrified to express his joy.
But when you sleep, he comes out to play,
In your wonderful dreams.

The images you protect,
Are cartoons you picked up and maintain,
Without which we would have a relationship.
Everytime I try to feed you medicine of love,
You pick those crusty scabs of fear,
that never heal.

As miserable as this path has been,
My love for you has continued to grow.
If you'll just step out from that cloud
and into My Light,
We'll laugh at all this bullshit.

~ Healing Wolf ~

My Tree in the Garden

~

In the field of hope Grandmother Spirit and I sat and turned up the rich black soil so it could feel the warmth of a spring day. My hands dug small tracks in the dirt and for two days I knew the toil over land. On the second day my hands touched some rough thing beneath the surface, I pulled it out and examined it in the light. It was a shriveled old seed, I started to through it over my shoulder but grandmothers voice stayed my hand "what is it" she asked, "a seed" I replied, "plant it" she said. I started to protest but her stern eyes caught me and I grew silent, I put it in my neck pouch but then her voice came again "plant it now" she instructed, angrily I got up and stalked off to the garden where I grew my medicinal herb's. why should I plant it here I wondered, I don't know what it is, it could kill my whole garden I thought. I wrestled with the notion on not planting it and saying I had. no, the truth would come out, so I planted it in a corner of my garden in a deep hole, I poured compost on top of it and watered it. There stupid seed grow out of that hole and you deserve to live. I challenged and tested that seed from the start. I returned to the field. A week passed and I went to weed my garden. I was shocked, there in the corner stood a small sapling tree. I raced to check the ground. This was weird, I had been tricked somehow by someone. I watched and time passed. The sapling grew all spring and summer. Now it shaded the garden on the hottest parts of the day, my garden flourished and grew. One night I sat with grandmother spirit and asked her about the tree, she told me to go check it in the morning and wouldn't speak of it anymore. I woke up and made my way to the garden, all of the leaves of my tree had fallen to the ground as the cold season had started to approach. I stared hard at my tree, so barren, then I noticed something fall from a low hanging branch to the earth, I walked over and picked it up. It was rough and withered and shrunken, an exact replica of the one I had planted. a feeling stole over me I'd never felt before, I felt complete.

~ *King Mongoose* ~

Untitled

ᴕ

A Painted King, A Lion Who Catches fire, A Healing Wolf with Vision
Awe inspiring in their majesty While cynical herds graze upon the plains
of delusion Here there is Awakening these dull embers fanned to life by
Spirit. Reborn through the portal of desperation healing and sacred med-
icine Compassion in a world of pain Inner alchemy, vision and intention
Trust in a powerful Spirit A silent flame witness to an ugly facet of human
condition Suffering fruit born from a tree of sadistic roots
Storm of Spirit, shattering the bands of attachment the living and dead
welcomed to this chronic feast Whither away now Delight in the presence
of now being in the moment A mystical time, a sacred place, transforma-
tion. Underway, a cohesive blend of tradition
Birthing peace…wisdom This world is all illusion, life is pain Stolen land,
stolen people Paradox is the land of the free, free to be homeless faceless,
free to starve, free to die
Blind mankind twist a gift With libertine lives of perversion divinity
rediscovered beneath starry heavenly light arms uplifted skyclad, Divine
Mother's embrace.
Skyfather's blessing. This monologue has heart
Kingly fools & divinely appointed monarchies, feeding on the deluded
herd drunk with the blood of innocence, professing piety among men
The Ninth Circle awaits you, indestructible, immortal spirit of man
This power to adapt within any given circumstance, for better or worse.
In clarity there is no deceit Fuck the NWO, UN, WTO, CIA, DEA, ATF,
FBI BOP, CDC, & ABC, NBC, & CBS. Anything and anyone telling me
what to believe, who to believe, when to act How to think, live, & feel,
especially the CCPOA. Which is the bile in the belly of this beast
Fuck you! Seraphim above and below, do what thou will is the law.
The consequences of which, each man bears alone freewill. Think for
yourself & live to create & love listen & you may hear
Your own inner Wizard speak.

~ Loving Eagle ~

A Walk in the Garden

❧

I walk into the garden and am transported to a new world. Lotus petals drift form the sky like rain and cherry blossoms fallen to the ground form great chains to dance with the wind like snakes. The sun is hot and steamy, it drifts through in patches of light pushed by the shoulder of the wind. In the center of the garden is a fountain, standing atop the highest tier the voodoo priest and the monk play chess. I call out to them and the voodoo priest stands grabs his staff and hurls it at me, it embeds itself at my feet and stares me face to face, the red skull and crow feathers less frightening up close on its knobby perch. I side-step and call again, the monks stands and grabs his staff to hurl it at my feet, it too embeds itself in the ground and I stare at the now lifeless serpent coiled atop tin covered in gold inlay. I turn away and leave them to their game of kings.

I notice an elderly couple walking down a shaded aisleway of trees. I rush after them and catching up to them I interrupt their conversation. I ask their identities and am awed to hear the replies of grandfather sky and mother nature, I ask if they are gods and they laugh until tears roll down their ageless faces. No, they tell me they are merely keepers of a way. I leave them to explore more of the garden. I find a flagstone patio with a small bench surrounded by a hedge. I enter the alcove and find a small child sitting on the bench swinging her feet through the air and singing. I sit next to her and quietly she looks up at me, I want to ask her why she is alone but the question is forgotten on my lips as she stares at me with the deepest ocean blue eyes I have ever seen. She reaches out and takes

my hand curling it into a fist and she kisses my knuck-
les, her breath is warm. She turns my hand over and
begins prying my fingers apart uncurling them into a
flat palm. There in my palm is a single flame licking
the air like a serpentine tongue. I stare into the flame
and the maya of my life unfolds, I watch things of old
and new then the flame sputters and dies. I am startled
to find myself alone, I stare at my palm again and wish,
nothing comes. It begins to rain rose petals, I watch
them cover the ground in a red blanket. I get up and
make my way to the gate. I walk briskly and when I
reach the gate I step through and pull the bars closed
behind me. I reach into my shirtfront for the key, I
pull it out and it gleams in the light. I let it go and it
chinks against its chain and my chest. I push the gates
wide open and snatch the key from my neck snapping
the chain, I hurl it into the garden out of sight and it
disappears into the undergrowth and I turn to walk
down the pathway backout into the world.

~ *King Mongoose* ~

At the Edge

❧

At the edge of insanity
Where I fight my battles…
Going to that dreaded place of many forms
In a second everything can turn into chaos
Trying to keep balance in this wilderness is a constant fight
My old insecurities have all reawaken.
Everything I work so hard to keep from the world is out playing
With assurance of no regrets that it doesn't matter
What happens while I'm there lost in my own realm.
Sometimes in the midst of this madness I find clarity
My emotions are far from being in balance
My anger boils
And melts with the calmness
I try to display
I am a man!
A human form–
Bound by my own limited flesh and thoughts
I see the world
Not as a lost paradise
I see it
With my own realities,
My own judgments
My own shortcomings;
-Sometimes-
I wish I could release
Mankind of all suffering
Other times,
I hate with such a terrifying force
That it doesn't matter reason exists within
That–
I am, part of the mystery.

~ *Fierce Fox* ~

Society

*

Trapped in our society's social order
of how we are supposed to behave
leaves me to live his order
for me to be accepted.

Who is Society?
I have never met him.
Is it Government? Religion?
Or even your parents and peers?
When they tell me to act this way
or that way
you're looking foolish
you shouldn't do that
feel that
be that way.

I have found most recently
thanks to Manny and the Group
that if I take a risk to do something
against our Society's order,
risk looking foolish
childish
odd
that for me the reward of feeling pure joy
exhilaration
happy
is worth it to me.

~ Unknown ~

To: All Men in Search of Miracles

❧

Maybe-
If I stripped these rags
called skin, and show you that underneath it all
we have the same color...
Probably you'd believe me then,
that the same infections running through your veins
run in my own...
And if still it is not clear enough
I'll go deeper
and take each strand of muscle off
my bare body,
to expose the roots of my bones
the cells of my blood, my genetic make-up:
everything that makes me a human being.
Maybe this will prove once and for all, that I am
just like you...
Lost in a foreign land so far from my beginnings.
Almost all that is painful to you creates the same rupture in my heart.
Every deception you have given or received I had.
I also came from the union of love or passion as you did.
But I am one with you;
A nomadic invader of this concrete box
a sorrowful soul looking for answers
a volunteer to my own insanity.
Miracles don't come easy in here
But I've found one
One that keeps giving,
feeding our hungry soul lost in their own grief.
I've stopped trying to make sense of what you are
because it is clear to me now
You are what you are...
A colorless sphere of compassion
A big paradox
Of godly might.

~ Fierce Fox ~

Traveler

~

Weary traveler where do you seek to be?
Mind if I ask what possessed you to leave all you have?
Why would you travel through this harsh and brutal landscape
when this road would have sufficed?
Did you not have everything to your hearts content?
Kind sir I do not mind, but I am tired and hungry, will you
nourish my body?
I will tell you the tale of my life if you will lend me a bed
to sleep.
I have little but what I have is yours, so tell me.
Kind sir I was cast away for I was diseased, unwanted.
I made my trek along these barren lands and after years of
wandering you were the first to invite me into your humble
home.
Stranger what disease would have you casted about?
What ailment should you have that could not be cured?
My affliction is earthly, I wither as a tree with no roots, I
with no past seek my future.
Young man your suffering is well within yourself, look into this
fire that I have made and cast your worn and tattered shoes
in there.
Watch them burn and your past is revealed.
I watched until the last embers died out.
Broken out of my reverie, I scan the grounds.
Empty silence with only brown sparrows chirping.
The kind old man was gone, but in his little abode there were
pictures of all I have known.
And above the fire place on the mantel was pictures of us, a
baby in a crib, a boy with his red ball, a teenager
graduating junior high, the next one was of me as a man.
I was transfixed and knew that next picture frames were of me as
an old man.
The same old man that gave me food, heat, and a bed to sleep.

~ *Dancing Cobra* ~

Sanctuary

❦

Weekly I walk through the hate.
Like sweat, it drips off my armor.
The fear is caked on it like mud
and the sadness quietly sobs.
All these plates of armor
clang as I strip at the door.
Entering into the sanctuary
I witness eyes alive with love,
faces shining with smiles
and relief that we're still here
to brave the tortuous beauty of growth,
birthing the true self of our hearts.
These truths are hidden
but in the sanctuary, their beauty
is revealed.
The hope of these undeniable truths
blossom and grow
even among the pain and doubt.
The essence of each individual of
The Circle
has created this magic
…of healing.

~ Healing Wolf ~

The Clown of Passionate Compassion

❧

Worn out, fatigued and drained,
from his sick bed he came.
Inside the Circle he sat,
straining to work with Spirit.
He keeps the flame of hope alive,
which he got from our friend,
who crossed over to the other side.
You know, where souls know their real name,
and death is alive with peace.
He brings Elders to light our paths,
preparing us all for wheel barrel rides.
Tirelessly he walks the wire,
coming back as long as they let'em,
relentlessly fighting to get inside.
The Clown of Passionate Compassion.
Inside our Circle lives his fire,
deeply pained by our suffering,
unyielding in his desire
the path he chose is ours,
we share,
leading us all from behind.

~ Healing Wolf ~

Untitled Number Six

～

vows of silence in cold rooms
where winter cracks the frozen eaves and humble minds
regard with awe the spider's web across the clean translucent sill.
a morning song of gravest joy resounds through halls
clean-swept and dark while from the flume
of coarse red brick the lazy smoke of manzanita
snakes into the still silver sky of dawn.

my heart reaches not for flesh and blood
or noisy city storefronts;
not for beats of hearts of lifted hands,
bland faces in garish clothes
or the babbling unity of anxious minds.

my heart reaches for the vow,
for morning songs and simple wonder,
for meaning when my hands create
food and warmth instead of words
and futile forms that anguished grieve
to be revealed at my soul's cost.

~ *Shaman's Key* ~

The Letter

This is a letter to the members of the men's support group. I want you to know I see your hunger to grow into the men you long to be. Your efforts to grow provides me with the hope I need to become the man I long to be.

I want to remind you that the path we have chosen is in no way an easy one. However I know that we are strong enough to fulfill our desire to become men of honor as well as integrity.

It is up to only us to be able to give the gift of growth to our brothers who will come after us. We my brothers are the teachers of tomorrow and it is up to us to teach ourselves what we must know in order to be good teachers.

Think how lost we would have been if men like Rob, Don, Bob and Dennis would not of taken the time to learn how to help us grow. We were lucky to have men willing to accept us for who and more importantly how we were. Now it is our turn to stop judging each other and learn how to help our brothers grow.

This is the time to boldly embrace the fact that we are leaders in this stone world we live in. And we as men can make a place where men can be men without having to kill each other over race, politics and petty amounts of dope.

With the utmost respect your brother.

~ Painted King ~

The Inside Circle Training

֍

The Inside Circle training is something my words can hardly explain,
grateful to be one of sixty men sitting in a circle
surrounded by an energy so strong it takes your breath.
The soft, the kind, the gentle of some, to the dangerous and fearless
men…
who in the blink of an eye will silence you forever if not careful!!
This is the caliber of men, if you dare to sit with.
The energy so raw your stomach will churn and send the message:
Caution!! I'm rattled and shaken to step forward into the fiery circle
that holds the strongest of men. (So)…stay quiet and hide, and watch
what happens. Hey you !!Yeah you!! Sixty pairs of eyes pierce my soul
and shattered my armor in one quick second. Weak and scared, I drop
to my knees completely naked, for all the men to see. From across the
room, I hear with a thousand echoes…Yeah You!! Down There!!
Those words ring and ring, but down on my knees I wait and wait…
My time has come!
All that I held so dear is gone. The mask, chest plate and the fucking
horse I rode in on, GONE!
On my knees, the words still ring, Yeah You! Down There!
With no armor now, I become what I hate the most…a victim.
The tears fall, my knees knock and my heart cannot hang anymore.
Just get it over with already!!
A gentle hand rubs my back and a soft voice whispers in my ear…
"Yeah you, down here…it's OK."
I raise my hand to see my guardian angel, who came down from above
to protect me. The tears stop, my vision clears and there is no angel.
The soft voice sweeps my ears again… "What do you see?"
What seems to be a thousand kings down on their knees,
each with their gleaming sword drawn for my protection & comfort.
The gentle voice echoes once more…
"Welcome my son, to the Inside Circle…
of the strongest warriors known to man!"

~ *Unknown* ~

Untitled Number Four

᷇

I am driven to seek the truth you fiend
and my love cannot be demolished by any demonic demons
that has fantastically appeared from out of the emptiness of my flesh,
but let me endure its piercing claws
drawing blood from a drug addicted fix.
So I confess all my clandestine action to come to light
that my love may be driven to its limits of possibilities.
Cautiously aware of any stares looked upon me as a madman.
You fantastic demonic fiend driven to demolish the truth
which I have endured in the flesh.
Confess now and I will give you your fix
so you can once again love me clandestinely.
You are the maven of emptiness,
but I will not be driven from my own dominion.

~ Dancing Cobra ~

A Reckoning With Myself

❧

There have been many great thinkers and strategists of the world and depending on which segment of history you choose to review the names are synonymous with meaning; Aristotle, Julius Caesar, Genghis Khan and Ramses, to name a few and bearing in mind the greatness of all their worldly travels, coming in contact with all the different colors of humanity, I am stricken with puzzlement that in all their tales of travel they never recite or speak of man's uncertainties or vulnerabilities.

Most speak only of their strengths and deeds of mighty labor and conquests. After pondering this picture my initial reaction was one of sadness which subsided after remembering histories fond saying, "Let's repeat ourselves." The very fact that we are here in this room is reaffirmation of this saying. We take our turns on the revolving axis of time, but in our travels vulnerability is spoken and hopefully remembered.

In this room beholds a body of greatness and a forum of priceless memories. You men here have empowered me to be the man I thought I was being all along. But I found out I had only been scratching the surface. At the end of each day here I've always professed something to you and once again, men, I have that headache! Everyone can identify with that headache because it's like banging your head with a hammer when it stops it feels so good!

I am in this prison as a sentenced man by society. By faces in robes who professed their greatness over me while sitting on their judgmental benches. They attempted to silence my allied voices and screams of the truth by saying, "I hold you in contempt!" I then smile and say, "Say, the feeling is very fucking mutual!"

So I say to you and now, if I am to be judge, let it not be from hypocrites or social interests, let it be from a forum of respect, character and shared dignity. You multitude of men you honor me with your commitment from within. Your sacrifice is not weighed by wealth because the value of these sweat and elements is greater than an orgasm!

I walked in here thinking I was a well rounded full man, but, half a man was I really. I've turned myself inside out trying to gain the answers to all my youthful longings, and just like everyone else here, just when we think we trust ourselves implicitly and we've got it all wrapped up and figured out the miracles of our medicine begs to differ!

How frightening and unsettling it must be to have a rug snatched out from under that portfolio of smugness and arrogance that you claim is you! The portrait of our Picassos' suddenly seem like ogres and beasts. And as we struggle with trying to regain our vision and focus of who we thought we were, the painful reality won't allow us to have that same painting. Even though the taste was bitter and the virgin sight gruesome our new painters brush and glasses show us the beauty of each new creation. With these portraits we realize that we must feel our vulnerabilities and even lose a little dignity in order to be painted in a manner that is dignified.

I say to you Pat, you are to be honored this day at the forefront of our continuing legacy. Each man in this room has a tremendous obligation, a duty to carry the dream, acknowledge the dragon in it's full throng and carry it's fire to the nostrils of ourselves and the unassuming as well. I love the men in this room. I could never say good-bye to your memories, so, I'll just hold them here in my heart and take them with me back to my life.

~ York / Wise Tiger ~

Untitled Number Two

For a few brief moments,

I touched the sacred.

With laughing tears,

I felt released.

All my life I've misinterpreted

the language of emotions.

I was proud of my foolish misunderstandings.

While aggressively defending my stupidity,

I thoughtlessly crushed all else but my own.

I move a little more carefully now.

I want to touch the sacred again,

Maybe a little longer next time???

~ Healing Wolf ~

Untitled Number Six

~

Here's the consequence of your existence,

You must come back to me.

How you do that is up to you.

It can take a long time or a short time.

By way of hard experience,

or wisdom by observation.

You can get out of your own way,

or remain your greatest obstacle.

These are the reasons I gave you free will.

You will come home to Me, child of Mine.

The hard way or the easy way.

If you'll listen,

I'll show you,

The way of indescribable joy.

If you reject My advice,

your path will be full of poison.

~ Healing Wolf ~

Death Grip

Weary was the man
driving through no-mans land
outside Folsom Prison.
Off the road
in the dry brown grass
something mystical unfolded.
He pulled over, and
underneath his weariness
his spirit came alive.
Standing tall
eye terrified
a red tailed hawk gripped
a large garter snake in its claws, which wrapped itself
twice around his neck and once around his wing.
Squatting next to these magnificent creatures
locked in this death grip at the edge of mortality
that Lion caught fire.
He picks up the snake's tail and gently begins
the impossible,
coaxing her to relax her death grip on the hawk.
His soft murmuring voice and concentration
is unaffected by the prison authority
who crashes harshly and loudly onto the scene;
she's instantly muted and transfixed
by witnessing the impossible.
In these magic moments
the Lion slowly convinces these two powerful creatures
to retreat from the brink of death
until they both feel
released
and bolt away to freedom.
Leaving that weary Spiritual Lion
blessed to have caught fire
again.

~ Healing Wolf ~

The Battle

❧

Messenger and transmutation
locked in a battle by the unexpected.
Action and reaction,
now without divine intervention
the message is lost;
transmutation will change no more.
What force lives on this plane that
can seduce the release of
transmutations serpentine grip?
What power prowls the planet
that can remove the messengers
sharp ebony talons that cut and rip?
As the lion of fire exits the savanna
of tortured souls he comes upon
the death dance of
transmutation
and the message.
Set ablaze by his passionate compassion
he tenderly takes hold
and starts to make a change in the outcome.
With kindness and devotion
he untangles
deaths knot.
Quietly talking and teaching
in his shamanistic manner.
Showing both hawk the message
and snake of transmutation
a new way.
Only in
surrendering to trust
will they live past this day.
Once more the lion has caught fire
and saved lives
with his love.

~ *Painted King* ~

Differences
❧

Reading the best books about sex

is not the same as her musky smell

inflaming your lust.

Tasting her delicious flavor

on your lips.

Feeling the heat of her hot flesh

rub and pound against your wanting.

Hearing the ecstasy of her shrieks

and satisfaction of her groans.

Seeing all this ecstasy simultaneously

gives the experience of living it.

So practicing all that stuff by yourself,

isn't the same as having a lover.

And it isn't the same

as getting on the rug

instead of talking about it.

~ Healing Wolf ~

Rays of Matter

A sparkle, a glisten and gleams, that illuminate from dreams.
the cascading of ever fading light,
A moment of stardom, a time to shine.
Where it's rays fail to show in the dark spaces,
of my heart and mind.
Despite the light I stand to shine in pursuit,
of effective vision.
I'm a passing image, a mere optical illusion,
of life's veneered confusion, in the borrowed,
extracted and recreated images that brings nothing
new under the sun.
Shine? Shine.
Not in the gloom where clouds of distraught,
depressing and desolate times hover above the short span of my life.

WHERE THE ONLY RAYS THAT MATTER...

Is the one that shone forth on a dark path of a lost soul
who would have stumbled to death.
Had they not been witness to that bright ray of hope
that is in you...
The rays that matter...

~ Courageus Tiger with Divine Compassion ~

I Seen with My Own Eyes

❧

I seen with my own eyes condemned men fly.
I seen with my own eyes confined men lift a roof with their hearts
and fly free among the trees and their own childhood.
I seen with my own eyes a tormented man given his innocence back.
I seen with my own eyes
a loving bull move a whole room with his desire to live free.
I seen a father dragon reclaim his heart.
I seen a buffalo wizard find his forgotten magic.
I saw with my own eyes a shaman find a lost child.
I saw with my eyes strong eagle wings
free his eaglets with a heart of a dove.
I seen with my eyes a little giant shake a stone prison.
I saw with my eyes dolphins with snakes and owls
stand in the same place at the same time
and they all knew they belonged there.
I seen with my eyes a healing wolf snap at a wise eagle
and the eagle did not fly away in fright or distrust.
I saw with my own eyes a holy man recall how to truly trust.
I seen with my eyes an angel land in the room refusing to be left behind.
I seen a young silver wolf care for his pack.
I saw a burning tiger uncaged himself.
I seen and never will forget a courageous loving bear find his power.
I seen with my eyes a man of many coats
defend his integrity with a fierceness
that shook stone pillars.
I felt with my heart a painted king's guilt
surgically removed by his tribe's magic.
I seen with my own eyes demons flee in the onslaught of hope.
I seen a loving father bear
learn to love himself
for who he is.
I seen for four whole days
with my heart not my eyes.

~ Painted King ~

Truth Circle

❧

I can not control what you get out
of the circle you sit in.
What I can control is
what I put into the circles I sit in
and therefore
what I get out of the circles I sit in.
I know for a fact that I only get
as much out of the circle as I put in to it.
And I can want the best in the world for you.
And that does not mean anything.
I long for the day that we all
reach deep into our hearts
and hold nothing back from each other.
Just think of the depth of a circle where we all
are willing to look at the truth
of the feelings we are feeling
right that second every second we sit there.
Can you see how healing a circle with such depth could be?
Can you feel the power in such a circle?
Are you willing to sit in this circle?
Now just think that nothing
except the truth of who you are is what you put in.
Race does not matter.
Religion does not matter.
Rather you are a man,
a women or even a child
just does not matter at all.
Only your truth matters.
So here we sit, just us with the opportunity
to touch each other's hearts
and maybe to sit with spirit
but only
if we are brave enough to tell the truth
of who we are and what we feel...

~ *Painted King* ~

Reaching

❧

I am reaching out to any one who can see that
I am reaching out for love.
I am reaching out for compassion but, mostly I am reaching out in
hopes Of being accepted.
I am reaching out to any one who can see.
I am reaching out to you and to every one who can see.
Do you see me reaching?
Can you see the hunger in my eyes?
Do you see your self reaching out?
Do you dare?
We are all reaching. And you know it.
I am reaching and you are reaching
And the whole damn world is reaching.
At the risk of looking like a fool will you still reach?
Will you take a chance of finding what you are reaching out for
By reaching out into the unknown?
I am willing to reach out and help you reach out.
I do not know what it is you are reaching out for
And it does not matter to me what it is you are reaching for.
I just want you to know that
You do not have to reach alone, just reach.
Reach when you can not do any thing else.
Never stop reaching reach for your life reach for your hopes.
Reach for your dreams.
Reach as if
Your life depended on you reaching.
Is it too much of a reach to think
That just maybe it does?
So reach and keep reaching;
And if we all reach
And keep reaching
We may just be able to
Wrap our hands around what it is we are reaching for.

~ Painted King ~

What I Give the World

❧

What I give the world is just
What the world gives
Back to me.
I can not expect goodness
From others
Until I give goodness
For the mere sake of
Goodness.
I can not see growth
Until I first am willing to grow,
Nor can I see
Contentment until
I live with contentment.
Until I can fully grasp
That all I need
Is here right now
I must be content always
Looking away from
Where I am.
If I can not find joy or bliss
In this second
Then tomorrow will only bring
More of the same
Discontentment.
All I have or need in this world
Is right this second.
What else could I need to touch my soul
And be content?
What I give my soul
Is just what my soul
Gives me.

~ Painted King ~

Greg

❧

Parting, parting with the ability to sit with you in this place at any given time.

Parting, parting with a friend who walks with honor parting with my brother.

Parting, parting with the humor you bring here,

Parting with your doses of glee.

Parting, parting with a man who will move out over the world in a good way.

Parting, parting so you can go teach the children of tomorrow's greatness.

Parting, parting is only one step in the direction you must take

to make your life matter to others as much as it matters to me.

Part well my brother.

Our friendship has no parting that un-binds us;

we are forever bound by what we share.

Parting, parting is just one more step

in your great life.

~ Painted King ~

June - Month Six

SHADOW, WOUNDS, RUG-RIDES, RANTINGS

I do what I do in defense against myself and to hide my fear of living defenseless against myself. What's hidden beneath the flesh can be etched in the skin. The demon in the darkest corners of the mind went from protector to destroyer of the fragile wounded child. This destroyer is confident in miserable satisfaction and ancient imperfection, completely unconscious of their interactions.

This destroyer is the shadow called denial, the constant companion of mismatched emotions. It laughs at good and feeds the perversions of charlatans. They are the many ugly faces of me.

Life's pressures lead to insanity for the young, without eldership and to begin the fearless moral inventory of passionate compassion and healing of wounds. The blankets of fear, smothering truth, must be removed to begin believing in ourselves again through love—self-love.

Without the One, victory can have a rotting stench. This can be the nightmare, many plead to God to escape and fall into painful projections for what they believe is His unresponsiveness.

Sacred space is created with ritual and initiation to learn how to discover and deal with shadows. In the Circles elders protect the way towards maturing for men of all ages. Once men take the ride on the rug to heal, the ride cannot be undone, the bell cannot be unrung.

Stone–Man

☙

A strange thing happened to me the other day, I was hiking the back country deep in an ancient old growth forest.

It was a beautiful day the sun filtered through the tops of the trees like melting honey. And a soft breeze whispered a haunting melody as it tickled the back of my neck.

The air I took into my lungs was sweet like spring flowers and I could hear the sounds of birds singing close by. And the small creek that ran close to the trial was as pure and clean as any water I had ever seen in my life.

I hiked for miles and miles enjoying the raw beauty of the earth and what it meant to be alive and free on this special day.

But as I followed this trail everything began to change; the tree's became much larger, they were giants and choked out the sun. It was a dark place and a cold feeling stirred in the pit of my stomach.

There was no sound, completely silent, the air smelled old and stuffy and even the creek was still and didn't move. Even though I was a little scared and extremely nervous I continued along the trail.

When out of nowhere a large owl swoops down across the trail right in front of me, drops a black stone about the size of your fist on the trial.

Then the owl lands on a branch in an old dead tree and watched me. Spinning his head left and right, he calls to me in a ghost like hooo-hooo-hooo. The owl says to me; Pick up the stone and see your future.

So I did as he asked and I picked up the stone and when I did I could feel the weight of tormented souls. And even though the stone was black I could see inside of it.

There inside was a sight that frightened me all the way to the marrow of my bones. There locked inside of this black stone was a man but there was something wrong, something strange.

It looked like two men facing away from each other and their backs were grown together. One facing one way and the other facing the opposite way.

But even stranger than that was even though there seemed to be two, they were actually the same man. One had a kind face and when I looked into his eyes, I could see that he was a good compassionate human being.

But the other face was angry and he spit out hate and he screamed as he kicked his legs and swung his arms. It was two sides of the same man and they hated each other. And they battled hard, one leaning forward so that his opposite was off balance with legs and arms in the air.

Then when one was too tired to hold the other off balance, his opposite would do the same to him. This went on and on inside their stone prison. I was horrified at the sight of this man trapped inside this stone, at war with himself.

I looked up at the owl and asked him, "Why is this man being treated this way?" the owl says hooo-hooo that man committed a crime and society placed him in front of a witch wearing a black robe they call a judge.

Now he is condemned to live his life in stone and anything he ever does which is good will be forever over-shadowed by his one bad deed. He must live with his worst enemy, himself.

"Why are you showing me this? I yelled at the owl," and who the hell are you anyway?

"Hooo-hooo-hooo because the witch wearing the black robe has sent me here for you." Hooo-hooo I am the keeper of the stone-man.

Then the owl lifted his wing and there tucked away in his feathers was another black stone. He says to me, hooo0hooo this stone here is for you. I screamed and threw the stone I had in my hand at the owl as hard as I could. But he easily caught it in his massive talons.

Then he swooped down from the branch and landed hard on my body. I tried to fight him off but it was no use. The owl stuffed me inside a black stone.

Beware of witches wearing Black Robes.

~ Indio ~

Untitled Number Two

~

Some men's lives

are printed in the skin

in crowsfeet and crevasses,

in the weary knowing slant

of shielded eyes;

chapters indelibly written

scrawled in the dark

by life, by choices,

by all that's hidden beneath the flesh,

by what's been broken and healed over,

unhealed, neglected

praised in the light

and dis-honored in darkness

until the tattered canvas

can no longer hold the paint.

~ Shaman's Key ~

Crazy Tyrant

The crazy tyrant in my head
constantly criticizes
repeatedly condemns
and hates being disagreed with.

He pulls up all my flowers,
blossoms of humility and compassion,
planting weeds of pride and anger
poisoning all he touches.

~ Healing Wolf ~

Strings

The stage is set, props stand within reach of those who would wield them. The puppeteer above checks his marionette strings one last time. All is well. The curtains part and the dance begins a whirling dervish of jerks and turns.

Imitation of life by one who has none. A mockery of truth. An illusion with the bare essentials. The strings almost invisible to the eye in the subdued light. The viewers forget they are there as the plot deepens and twists then arises to ensnare them for the duration. A trick of old. A cadence of movement increases, building to a climax accompanied by the music created in the mind. The fatal blow struck on stage. The hearts open with compassion. The energy electric and full. No longer a drama, but a real thing felt by real people. Love lost and found, death and tragedy. The tears flow and cease. The curtain falls. The crowd leaves silently dragging their severed strings behind them. The silent puppeteer watches them go with a knowing eye and smile.

~ King Mongoose ~

Untitled Number Two

❧

Open your eyes
Take in your surroundings
If you felt like me
You'd want to kill too
Trapped in my old life's memories
Counting the days since you've left
I've been screaming silently
Is it possible to wake up from myself
Drugs and violence don't scare me
It's molding me
Shaping me
Loving me
The only true feelings I have now
Hatred, rage
Pain's my only true friend
So far it's the only thing I've come here with
That's still with me
Like a sock in a dryer
I've been missing in action
I've gone to where the dirty socks go
You only miss them
When you use them
My emotions are mismatched.

~ Loving Leopard ~

Facing the Demon

❧

When I look deep into the depths of my rotted soul,
it scares the shit out of me.
And it angers me to see what I've become
and to feel what I have become.
When I do this work,
when I can force myself to fully surrender
to the emotion and the hidden feelings,
I wake up a demon.
And this demon has sat in pools of his own blood
and laughed a most demented laugh,
this demon has taken human lives,
for the simple twisted thrill of watching death.
So when I do this work,
I have to face this demon.
And this sick twisted demon scares me.
Under the demon I have found a wounded child,
who has been hurt in many ways by wounded people,
this little child is too gentle to protect himself.
Thus the demon was born.
This demon started out as a protector,
protecting the child from pain,
but after so many years of wounds being inflicted on him,
the wounds festered and rotted, the demon went insane.
He became a destroyer instead of a protector.
Now I have to do hard work.
I have to look deep into my soul,
I have to save the child. I have to face the demon.
For the past few years I have been at war,
and I have found the innocent child I once was.
That's why I'm here,
my demon is too big for me to beat on my own,
I need your help.
United we can destroy any demons.

~ *Painted King* ~

Restoration

~

Are the Warriors strong enough to endure the pain of their own weaknesses?

To understand the power obtained from illuminating shadows?

Brave fears by stepping into them?

Surrender to the revelations of these dark ugly truths?

Can they embrace the mysterious contradiction that being intentionally vulnerable is being less fragile?

To stop hiding in chaotic silence to avoid their work?

To find freedom by breaking the shackles of laziness?

To refuse to hide behind blame, fault finding and excuses?

To accept the truths of the past as inspiration for the choices of the future?

To see with new eyes into the shadows that held their mind in darkness?

We who are grateful for the ritual of sacred space.

~ Healing Wolf ~

The Intruder

❧

I am the pretender
the intruder...
But here is also the one
that is never heard.

The one that wants
to escape my grip.

I can't let him
show himself
he is too vulnerable
too loving-too kind
-Sometimes-
he's too much of a dreamer.

I hate it
when others talk good about him.
Can't they see?
I am tough,
not this other
I know he will live on
when I'm gone
And that is
just not fair.

~ Fierce Fox ~

The Shodow Magician

❧

The Shadow Magician,
Is a reptile with a three foot rattle,
Trying to work everyone.
The Manipulator, The Charlatan,
Boasting of his great learning,
Exotic cruelty and detached superiority.
He perversely crushes others enthusiasm,
Ambitiously pursues secret knowledge,
Craving the power it brings this evil sorcerer.
Withholding important details,
Causing the meltdown of inspiration,
Injuring all with his black magic,
He cuts off his own soul.
Now he's contemplating a Wheel Barrel Ride,
It could lead to sacred spaces,
Which restores wholeness,
And curses the deadliest diseases.
Maybe now he'll find his medicine;
In the magic of the Circle.

~ Healing Wolf ~

Years as a Clown

~ᔣ~

Someone told me, but I didn't listen.
It just didn't register as important.
Once, I read about it, but again it missed me.
Maybe I was distracted with myself?
I felt confident about ignoring it.
Hell I even gave bogus reasons,
Boasting about my purported position,
Supporting my arrogant assumptions.
Someone re-worded it later, again I ignored it.
Secure in my foolish ways of dissatisfaction.
Then fragments in different situations,
Began to filter through my arrogance,
About the power of the truths I'd heard.
I didn't connect the fragments,
Too few, too far apart, and too hard to assemble.
I spent the next years catching fragments,
Collecting them, but still not able to connect'em
I wanted to insist on proof,
Demanding examples, confident when not given.
Now I know what time it is,
It seems so simple, how could I, how did I,
Act so foolishly arrogant,
So I could be so miserable.
For soooo long???
It's, all about life's lessons.
I feel I've been squandering
My whole life away, and didn't know.
Now I can start passing the tests
And graduate from existing to living.

~ Healing Wolf ~

It

&

It dwells in the recesses of me unnamed, unspoken, and untamed. The residue of a primordial savage, it's wildness both exhilarating and deadly, honed by a millennia of tactics, tried and true. It's mystical shroud akin to a magicians robes, what secrets lie in gold flecked eyes? What ancient symphony does its heart beat to? In its imperfection, its flaws seem desirable traits, held in awe and mystique by less civilized men, warriors strive to embrace it and become it in battle, yet hide it from the ones they love. To touch it awakens forgotten senses and floods a newly created surreal world with texture and depth. a nirvana and eden for the beast where nothing makes sense except the ringing of steel on steel punctuated by high notes of metal sliding into flesh.

~ King Mongoose ~

One

⁓

Civilizations rise only to fall. Kings, emperors, sovereigns, and their lapdogs fade to obscurity and as the castles crumble and fortresses lie in ruin. The battlefields disappear and the bodies of the dead are ready to return from whence they came long after the smoke clears and the flag has fallen. Scavengers arrive to pick over the bodies of the dead that were curbed by the strife of men. Tales are told only to be forgotten through the ages. The voices of heroic deeds and glorious victories fade from history like a setting suns last light before nightfall steals its thunder. The victors seize the spoils of war and the conquers write the history of the defeated not knowing they carve their own gravestones as they do so. Men return to their families to resume life's struggle and spawn the children to feed the war machine of tomorrow's army. Blood spilt is blood created. Many cry out to a silent God but how can vengeance and peace be granted? Why shouldn't a god turn deaf ears to those who are not blind yet cannot see? Who can barely crawl but choose to race. The universal truth that echoes throughout time and space is one. It's sole existence and definition says I am, I exist, I am here, to defy me is to defy yourself, to destroy me is to destroy yourself, accept me and live. From corner to corner of reality it screams its presence to a cruel and unrepentant universe. From the one comes two and so on to infinity, anything less is not whole and is intangible, an antithesis, and an anathema to the one. I am the one to accept it and embrace life, reject it and embrace nothingness and death.

~ *King Mongoose* ~

Seed

❧

The seed if you could track its essence goes back to a time before yesterday and today it goes back to when what is now wasn't then. It began with a slight, real or imagined and the inability to voice and express the hurt and rage I felt was done. Instead I choked it down into that black pit inside me where I dump what I don't want to feel. Did I leave it there? No! I fed it and nourished it with hate and hindsight and fed it with light once and awhile. How did I do that? I disguised it and snuck it out to feel and be heard as violence. What is it? A bubbling blob of emotions so mixed up and unidentifiable as all the colors of the rainbow blended into one color, it threatens to burst like a water balloon touching a needle wetting everyone near. It is something that causes a knot in my throat, the corners of my vision to constrict and grow small, my eyes also water and my stomach does backflips, my hands clench into fists while my blood races. What will I do with it? I'll cope because that's what I did the first time, repeat the pattern because its hard to forge a new path through my heart. That unknown jungle where savage beasts roam and long for a taste of my precious blood, maybe I can talk about it soon, maybe not, maybe to you, maybe not, all I know is I don't want to feel it anymore.

~ King Mongoose ~

Blue

Lost in my reverie, I find myself wading through the deep end of the ocean. Floating face up, hoping God wakes up! Because of this nightmare He's dreaming of me. Have me swimming with the fishes in the murky sea deeply affected! My empty carcass stripped, gutted and heartless, pleading to who cares, while waiting for a reply from the barren air. Revive what is dead, love is only asleep in its dungeon bed. Release my soul from its chambers. I've lived in danger, been hurted and deserted, so I let go in anger. My thoughts were conceived in the womb, born with the concept of my doom. To live in agony, to survive all tragedies.

Nothing can compare or prepare on what has happened to me. Happiness eludes my clutch, so I bust back at life.

But is it enough to erase such a deep pain? Can I attain love again?

The question bombards my mind, with an answer so hard to find, because in my mind I'm a sleep walking talking humanoid with a conscious to suffer, inflicted with the disease to love you. I'm consumed with rage to do battle with my faceless demons when they escape from their cages.

Flip the pages of my revelation! I'm preordained a sinner, who have yet to figure the meaning of my existence. Who listens when I talk? Who answers when I question? Hoping I can get lost into your seduction, seduced by how your body functions. So let me begin letting my spirit descend. When it was pure and not obscure or tainted by the world.

I'm sure this is God's nightmare; to dream up this love affair, then tear me away from those I care. Stare at my life! Study my odyssey? See all the ghosts that haunt me and all the evil thoughts that bothers me. Take a shot at me and examine my exit wounds, while the fumes of blood hangs thick in the air, let me share with you my dreams, bare you my soul! Help me bury my past and give me a future to hold. It all unfolds now! The power to be free and fly! "God's nightmare of Me"…

~ *Dancing Cobra* ~

Somehing Not in Bill's Big Book

❧

He was full of spit
which meant
running his car into the porch,
breaking the old lady's jaw,
never hearing a damn word,
saying what he wanted
the way he wanted
to who he wanted
and then one day
he ran clean out of spit
and someone cracked his skull
with a japanese carjack
right out in front of a
halfway house for drunks
without a car or old lady
before he had the chance
to make a fearless moral inventory.

~ *Shaman's Key* ~

Untitled Number Five

~

Creative juices flow through music or whenever I choose to use it. If you haven't guessed, this is some new shit that I had to spit; to get rid of whatever was eating at me. Because those maggots won't let up, until they chew through my gut, and I'm grittin' my teeth just to bear the burden. It all started when I was a teenager hurting and my family were strangers unaware of all the dangers that threatened me, so I had to act insanely. To the point where doctors had to dull my senses with novocaine. I was called deranged, estranged from my love ones, so I picked up a gun and made it my own son. We were more like brothers. He'd spit in the streets and killed my very enemies. Made me wealthy but I had to live stealthy because those filthy pigs would love to jail me.

You can tell me if I'm a raving lunatic in need of a hug, but I'm far from sick. Maybe a desperate thug driven to find love. Close to the truth? Maybe not but it's all I got, least for now. But if something comes up I'll shout out and you'll definitely hear it aloud. Even if you're off somewhere in the distant, you'll hear my voice echo and bounce back down into this mad crowd. What's my infirmities? Plagued with sickly thoughts that turns my stomach from the acid burns.

Purely unconventional cure, when I have to rip out my lungs just to catch my breath and revive myself back from death. My best bet is to razor saw my chest and examine what's left of this hollowed out cadaver. But don't cut out my tongue, I'm not quite done talking yet. I was unsung, strung out from the drug that made me all numb. I can't feel nothing, my fingertips are bits of bones that can't grip.

And my bitch refuses to write because she's sick of this shit. Like I ain't, knowing her memories grow faint. and I'm here with way out scenarios running between my ears, writing my ever so dearest and it's clear from her silent response that she's moved on dancing to a new sound. And my other fear is my moms, only if she could hold on seven more years and I promise I'll never be gone…Now what else is wrong?

There's no weed to calm me down except for the reality that's staring at me now. I just might be alone with no place to call home. Living in split dimensions within the twilight zone. Knowing in my bones, I've grown to love the taste of decayed waste, and somehow my face seems out of place in the midst of this human race.

I can't break the thought I'm a part of this alien nation, whose ancestors are asians with slanted eyes, and a tint of brown to this skin and green ink to mark my existence and vouch for what my life has been. Tortured at the most, abandoned at the very least. I was robbed to no choose and then caged like a vicious beast. Tell me what you want from me, I'm just one man, with one stand, half crazy and half mad and sadly to say, the state raised me and I was the bad one out of seven babies.
So please listen, my creative juice is about to run out and my tongue is dried out from cotton mouth. So if you miss out on what I just said, you might as well be dead, because this is the first and last time this shit will ever be read.

~ *Dancing Cobra* ~

Untitled Number One

Sometime I feel like saying fuck-it
fuck-you and fuck the world.
I could scream it
until my lungs burst
and shake my fist
and stamp my foot
and bang my head
again and again and again
until the blood
rolls down and drips
off the tip of my nose
following the sweat
and the tears
I've shed
in the thousand years
I've been here
and fuck it
'cause it don't mean shit;
I'm just one
of thousands
doing the same thing
and I could cut my wrists
or o.d. on some bad shit
and it wouldn't change a thing
I'd still be here
screaming in scribbled letters
my frustrations and fears
and fuck you for reading this
thinking you know what I'm saying
Just 'cause you don't know shit.

just fuck it man,
turn the page.

~ *Unknown* ~

Untitled Number Two

&

I have this little man in my head
hiding somewhere in the darkness
where I'm afraid to look;
a little green flicker
or maybe blue; who knows?
I think green, the color of jealousy, envy.
He is jealous of
what I am capable of and envies me
for trying to be better than I am.
I don't know how the fuck he got there
and is good at making his thoughts seem like my own,
constantly fucking with my head,
telling me I'm no good or not good enough;
people will laugh at me if I do my way.
I'm safer listening.
He's there, alright.
He's whispering in my ear right now:
I'm not a poet and never will be.
I can't even write a fucking letter.
Yes, he's good.
But he's scared.
That's why he hides in the darkest corners of my mind,
where I haven't looked in a long, long time.
But I'm starting to peek into those corners now,
scared as I am of the creviced darkness;
I can't wait to catch that little fucker
and shut him up
for good.

~ Unknown ~

It May Seem

꙳

It may seem to some that I am a poet
because I write
or a musician because I play
or maybe an artist or not,
if you have seen my work.
I'm none of these things.
I do what I do in defense against myself
and everything that is dark and ugly inside me.
I've tried to draw the darkness out and trap it on paper
but there isn't enough ink.
I thought I could expose the ugliness with words
to the light for all to see;
only it scurries deeper into the darkness and hides.
I've tried like the pied piper to draw them both out
and lose them in melodic tones
of perfect fifths and minor thirds
and they danced with heavy feet
on all my efforts.
I'm tired now, weak,
losing ground that I fought hard for
and I laugh now in the face of Death,
a mask to hide my fear
of living defenseless
against myself.

~ Unknown ~

Looking Back

❧

Teeth yellowed and weathered,
long before their time, work
to gnaw the tender flesh inside
his left cheek, a habit learned
early, seeing his mother knocked
unconscious one Spring day and
dragged limp across the fenced–
in lawn wet with morning dew by
her thick auburn mane twisted in
a knot of white scarred knuckles;
back into the kitchen she fled
to escape the rage that boiled
out of control.

Eyes, cold lead pools once hazel,
hooded by years filled with hate;
rarely now does light dance off
the callousness that pits the heart,
yet in this inhumane place he's
just one of many monsters kept
under lock and key.

~ Patrick Nolan ~

The Lonely Children

When I hear them cry, it makes me sad.
The lonely children who aren't so bad.
They're walkin' around with heads hung low.
Having no peace, no place to go.
On the streets, tryin' to be tough
But deep inside, they know it's rough.
Coming from shattered homes, dressed in rags,
Having no love and always getting tagged.
The lonely children with a chip on their shoulder
Living on the streets ain't easy at all.
What they want is a chance like you and me
The lonely children just want to be free.
They come in scared to a house of pain
Never know if they'll make it to the next day.
Runnin' away because they cannot play,
It's in and out of a nightmare play.
Getting beat up with belts and bats
Half the time, they don't know where they're at.
Always looking down down because they can't look up

Daddy's drinkin' beer, there's no milk in their cup.
Looking for love with hungry hearts
Chasing a dream that's in the dark.
They start doing dope to stop their pain
And get locked up; tell me who's to blame?
All they want is a chance to prove
That lonely children can be Presidents, too.
But that won't happen if we turn our backs
'Cause the lonely children just might attack.
Lonely children, lonely children, lonely children,
lonely children just want to be free.
Just give them a hug today and tuck them into bed
A little love goes a long, long way for a lonely child.
Lonely children, lonely children, lonely children,
lonely children just to be loved.

~ Unknown ~

Ok, I Get It

❧

Ok I get it. I'm here to feed my soul,
there is no other reason I walked through the door.
And it don't matter what I tell myself,
truth is I'm here to feed.

I'm here to feed me and to feed you
and to feed any man in this room
and it don't matter to me who fixes the meal
I just need to be fed.

So let's not pretend we don't know why we're here
we all know...

If we didn't we would not be sitting here
looking around to see who it is that's
gonna have the balls to fix the first
part of our feast.

~ Painted King ~

Hunting Rabbits

The snow is deeper when you're ten,
holding a 12-gauge on a rabbit a few feet away.
It knows you know its heart pounds
as the snow around its body melts,
waiting for that moment when all is silent.
The wind has pierced the trees
to the bone; two small thumbs cock
back the hammer:
Why isn't it home with its family,
out of the cold and sights of things
that want it dead?

~ Patrick Nolan ~

A Brief Discourse on Related Dynamics in Inner-Work Poetry

~

this is the process,
the excess, on into
the recess, the pit,
the bad-ass abyss,
where the things you thought
you killed all got wings
and stings, like wasps,
and you remember
you better remember
that childhood day
when you got stupid
and took a fig tree stick
to that grey paper nest
under the cobwebbed eave
then screamed like a girl
for a block and a half
because they ain't bees
and they don't die
and they don't give a fuck
about you being stupid.

~ Shaman's Key ~

It's Only Me

Yes, it's me
the misery, the anger, the dissolution, the hatred.
Yes
I brought all to you
I took what you gave
I laughed at your hopes
I stole your dreams
I stole your smiles
I scarred your soul
Yes me...
no, it's not the devil or any beast from down below
It's me—no, there are no reasons
No, there are no apologies, no, there are no excuses
It's only me I can't feel what others live for.
Don't expect me to explain, I don't give reasons,
I give pain, I give confusion.
Yes! I'm human, my mark you couldn't erase suffering
I now claim my cowardice I deny
My face I am afraid to show
Yes me, though I must say
it won't make any differences
My heart hurts, my spirit is gone.
these walls, I now call home
Yes me—walls that I see when my day begins
I try to look beyond but
my never ending tomorrow always reminds me of my faults...
A smile, I miss a hug I have to resist
After all I am all alone, trapped in my own demise.
Many lives I'd give if agony will forever
leave you in peace
Maybe, It's too late
Maybe, I am too afraid
Honesty certainly is not my trait.

~ *Fierce Fox* ~

Monstrum in Fronte, Monstrum in Animo
(Monster in Face, Monster in Soul)

In the cellar of my mind.
Cold, dank, Rats scurry
Through slime-filled
Crevices

Scratching out nests;
Breeding, feeding on decayed
Brain-stuff.

I scream for someone to turn
On the light.

the Rats scream with me…

~ Patrick Nolan ~

Untitled Number Nine

I feel like I fall forward into yesterday,
and backwards into tomorrow,
but all the time I'm flat on my butt in today.
What's said isn't what's meant.
What's expressed is covering up what's really going on.
Everything expected is said out loud,
But it's a front.
Covering up what should be said,
to break the choking strangle hold of fear,
Smothering the Angel called freedom.
then somebody changed the channel,
Or did I fall asleep?

~ Healing Wolf ~

If I Do This

There will be no turning back,
no second thoughts,
no twisting around the face
from the sun to shadow
like I've done and done and done
and there will be
no unsung heros,
and there will be no more regrets
and if I do this
I leave the barn door open
to the unreined foal
and every thing that wants to kill
can walk right out
and I could beat on the fuck'in mattress
but it wants blood my brother,
and it wants blood my brother.

~ Shaman's Key ~

Sign of Bullshit

*

Having an objection while sitting in the Circle,
objections requested, no-one speaks up,
to me that's bullshit.
Taking the same objection outside the Circle to voice it,
to me that's bullshit.
Double talking, like lawyers do,
to me that's bullshit.
Sitting in silence and not expressing wrongs,
to me that's bullshit.
Not being present when another warrior has the floor,
to me that's bullshit.
Not being present when a warrior has the rug,
to me that's bullshit.
Clowning during another warriors work,
to me that's bullshit.
Only speaking half truths when asked,
to me that's bullshit.
Not being accountable to commitments, agreements and responsibilities,
to me that's bullshit.
Using the excuse of knowing the process, not to work,
yeah,
to me that's bullshit too.

~ Healing Wolf ~

Priviliged Service

~

The mixtures of contagious poisons with heated emotions
produce nasty shadows.
Shadows that try to hide behind bogus virtue
which are transparent to the Clowns
pushing the wheel barrels.
Patiently they wait for the Warriors to get in
one at a time as many times as they want.
Inside the Circle, Clowns serve as guides of compassion.
They're not facilitators, they serve as facilitators.
Outside the Circle with armor on, Clowns too are broken.
Being in their medicine isn't a full time skill.
Shadows are powerful and clever.
They hunger to be fed, and are sometimes too quick.
But relentless are Clowns to see into the Shadows
revealing the misshapened and deformed creatures
that have deceived them and pulled out their fears.
Fears used as weapons to dominate and control
chased to unholy ground to hide with the liars, shadows that shamed
them into unspeakable acts.
Performed with unthinkable delight.
Shadows create riddles to avoid detection
from the loving compassion of the sacred Circle
held safe with confidentiality and truth
but very messy, splattered with spent emotions
draining as much poison as the Circle can heal
revealing the medicine and it's holy feel.

~ *Healing Wolf* ~

July - Month Seven

TRANSCENDING, SELF-DISCOVERY, CHANGING

Coming out of the darkness and beginning to walk in the life you want to live, means facing fears and to see clearly, errors, that stalk betrayal. This rebirth into peace and love begins to fill the empty spaces. This purification by pain transforms old darkness into new light, realizing how we evolve and change through integration.

Prior to being driven to the circles, we say anything to stay unchanged and broken. Usually we say "I don't care," and it's a mystery of what gets us to care. It's our brokenness that leads us to the circles.

The many steps to finding "it", begins in the circle as we learn the act of caring. There are many dangers when the soul begins racing for peace. Trust is built as we witnessed the shards of the smashed masks and broken shields of the elders who now guide along the path.

As I Journey Through the Labyrinth of Creation

As I journey through the labyrinth of creation.
I welcome you gentleman to vicariously participate in the strides!
–Stroll with me–
A bastard philosophy on the particulars of life.
A walk, a stalk unlike any witnessed throughout the archives of
human existence. A flow, A speech of eloquence in all it's fashions and
contentions. A purpose.
An insatiable drive stimulated through unparralleled persistence.
Enigmatic…idiosyncratic! Neo-manifestions of a jaded soul
thriving to make (what many only theorize about), happen!
As I synchronized undesirable to the blues of apathy, witnessed the
presence of lost personalities. Plagued by opacity…mirror image of an
escaped reality. Ranting & raving…repetitiously vexing me!
Refusing to depart leaving a vulnerable people in the gutter streets of a
dilapidated mentality. My people! Feel me! Paradoxical strides,
confusion and frustration frequently begging to escape these
complicated times. Wanna go…but I don't, wanna stay…and can't find
the strength to halt my own mobility. Pleading to bear the burden of
truth upon the youthful shoulders of I…Believing I'll survive.
Needing to live, yet accepting that I must die!
Martyrdom! Amongst the ancestral haven of all that is…shall I roam.
Reaching up to the skies.
Interrogating the universal order of creation.
Investigating the yin, questioning the yang.
Scrutinizing, conceptualizing, visualizing, constructing and materializing!
Communicating with forces of the uncomprehendables.
Striking and slashing at the ambiguities of this lifetime…
Face to face, Eye to eye, With the inconceivable.
Experiencing peace, and…essentially at war with all that is seen,
And unseen due to the enslavement of man.
Spiritual mounds of sand…
Foreign soil, and uncharted land!
–Stroll with me–

~ Shauka Mlimaja ~

Unknown
❧

Sometimes the burden of knowing
is so heavy.

It is as if I am walking
in and out of a maze.
Who builds these obstacles
that prevent me to reach
the core of my being?

I am stripped naked,
scared to find all the answers
to questions I dare not ask.

I cry...
for all those times spent
in hopeless wonder.

For prayers unheard
for miracles that never came.

What if this is
what it is meant to be.

I refuse...
to find the quest my life
has become

only exists in the mind of a fool.

~ Unknown ~

The Unknown Universe

❧

What is my ultimate goal in life? What defines me as a man? These
questions constantly
run wild in my mind.
This mind-unlimited vehicle of love, creativity, hatred and confusion, in
all; The maker
of my world.

Somewhere in it lies the "Understanding of Being."
For what are we without it? What a mysterious universe ourselves, so
close and
yet light years away from our reach. To understand, to reason, to journey
without
Fear - to reach known boundaries and go beyond their limits should be
in the aim
of our existence.
Life has an ending - no arguments about it; the more familiar I become
with this
fact, the more I learned death is not our enemy but an ally, not to be
ignored; it doesn't matter who, or what we believe ourselves to be,
death's hand will sooner or later caress us all.

The grandiosity, wealth, and sophistication of a king...the stench of
poverty, and ignorance, it's all irrelevant, when our time is up.

~ Heart of the Jaguar ~

Crying with Strangers

᷾

They came from the far reaches of the land, some closer, some far. Men from Oregon, Indiana, Illinois, Pennsylvania, New Jersey, NY, LA, Florida, England, Africa, even Australia, but just men…Almost forty men, old, men, young men, musicians, accountants, construction workers, to name a few. Fathers, sons uncles, nephews, brothers, cousins, G'pas and G'sons too…but just men. So here they came inside this California Prison, to spend most of four days with almost thirty prisoners…also just men. Big men, small men, old men, young men, many different cultures, backgrounds and stories. Fathers, sons, uncles, nephews, brothers, cousins, G'pas and G'son too…but just men. Almost seventy men in a prison chapel made up this congregation, a strange brew to stew…Why did they come is a wonder, as their voices are heard, prayer/song, in voices strong as thunder. The spirit of the truth overcoming all the obstacle's outside and within, within, within, within…So, what causes all these men to become, in this place that is a living hell for many? I was there…present…for the end I witnessed the miracle of Unconditional Love and the Spirit of the truth free many shackled, burdened hearts, including my own. And I am witness for JEHOVAH GOD, whose name means, "to cause to become", GOD of love and truth. I bear witness of the unforgiving being forgiven…by themselves, as the pain of the many filled the air, the Spirit chasing the demons away. I share the pain, tears, of sorrow and joy of all present, the hopes of the many that were strangers. Our tears have mingled and washed the strangeness away, crying with strangers, from the outside and inside, just men, strangers no more, who now live in my heart…strangers no more, one man at a time…

~ Loving Witness ~

Fear

☙

Strangled, paralyzed, jerk movements, clumsy, awkward and
brain locked.
Cold body shakes, sounds are distorted, static and silence clipped.
Unwanted conditions alive inside.
Unending, unwanted, and disguised.
These are not friends to embrace, understand or discover;
These disowned damaged parts are destroying me.
Brave it face to face, all monsters of mine,
Watch from the shadows as I stumble along.

~ Healing Wolf ~

Whiskers Bent – Whiskers Shaved

~

I stood in front of the little square mirror glued to the concrete wall in my cell this morning.

Thought to myself, another year gone past inside this place.

I looked into the eyes of the man staring back at me in the reflection.

He's growing old fast. His hair is turning gray and his look is distant and worn.

The years have taken their toll.

I know who he used to be, and I know who he want's to be, but who he is now is a mystery even to the one who shares his skin.

So I fill my sink with the water and grab a can of shaving cream and a fresh razor. Maybe if I shave off these old whiskers I'll recognize the man in the mirror.

I lather up my face real good and stroke by stroke, pull the razor across my face.

My mind begins to drift, thinking about the daughter I haven't seen in twelve years, about her mother, and about how crazy things used to be a long time ago, before I went crazy…

I think of all the missed opportunity and the man I could of been, the man I would of been and the man I am now.

When I finished shaving, I wiped my face with a towel and looked into the mirror, some of the whiskers were bent over and some of the whiskers were shaved off.

I looked worse now than when I started, kinda like my life.

~ Indio ~

It's Been So Long

It's been so long and yeah some how
I still shuffle along.
I spent years dwelling in the depths
of my own sorrow and despair. I stayed so
long I became comfortable there.
All along I know I didn't like it.
I didn't want it and feared it.
No matter how hard I looked it was the only
place I seemed to fit.
It was the only place where my
hate and darkness wasn't wrong. It's been
so long. So damn long
All them years I danced with
the gunners. I fought and stabbed but I never
looked at my fear.
I walked hard, fought hard
and felt right at home with a knife in my hand.
Everyday I became more of an animal and less a man.
It's been so long.
Out of the hole and back on the line.
Along came Pat and said there's something in your heart
that I know you can find.
He put me in a circle and said;
What do you see? As I heard each man speak
I knew there was hope for me.
It's been so long.
Now years later I smile, I laugh.
I shed tears & spend time with my fears.
I'm alive! I love, I feel shame,
I hug my brothers & I tell them my real name.
It's been so long
and now, I'm dancing right along.

~ *Healing Wolf* ~

On the Baptism of Christ

❧

What would you say of him
I mean as if you really knew him
standing eternally alone on that soft breaking bank of Jordan
stricken with truth, just then beginning to see,
to find the words to what is unutterable.

A flare from the sun bursting in a fiery lick
away and apart, free of the gravity that holds it, free,
before those same unutterable laws
allow it to die in cold space.

Stricken with the truth that what man can't control he kills.
The truth shall set you free, make you essence,
without wealth without family without fear, free,
the essence of man the essence of God.

He opens his mouth and stones are picked up;
he speaks, and the nails are driven through.
This he knows and it shows itself
in sorrowful, joyful lines etched deep into a face
far too young and far too human.

He steps into the brown idle river
flowing between two seas.
One is named "the Circle,"
the other Death.

~ *Shaman's Key* ~

Hate & Despair vs. Love & Hope

❧

Hate & despair are so much easier to live with than love & hope.
I know how to hate & I know how to hurt I have mastered the art.
Now that I allow myself to love
I see how much pain we can inflict on each other.

I'm scared shitless; can I bare it? So much pain
worn by the men I call brothers; tossed around like a hand grenade
with the pin pulled, in who's hands will it blow?
How many dreams will it kill when it goes off?

Will all my hopes be shattered like a bullet riddled windshield?
Will I find myself sitting in a puddle of my brother's blood
insane, screaming all alone?
Will my trust be peeled off my body like strips of flesh
to be carelessly tossed aside like trash? And
can I bare the sight of the brother I love holding the bloody pliers?

Is my word worth any more than the rotting corpse
I left in my wake? Or like the corpse
does my word turn to dust with the passing of time?

I'll tell you again my brothers
hate & despair is much easier to live with than love & hope.
Even knowing this fact I choose to love you.
Even knowing this fact I choose to hope…

~ Painted King ~

Armor

❧

I wear my armor proudly,
I keep it clean & polished…
I take my praise as I walk along in life
with my armor on…
all the people I meet say;
"That's nice armor you're wearing,"
and my chest swells up & I say,
"It's bullet proof & knife proof & nothing
can touch it or me."
"Where can I get armor like that?"
they all ask. I tell them:
You can't get this kind of armor, it was
crafted just for me by me…
I've worn this armor so long it fits like second skin,
I've worn it for so long it's made itself one with me.
I long to remove my armor & let the cleansing
light shine through & cleanse my soul
of the darkness I'm in…
Without my armor I'm vulnerable
to the cleansing light & that scares me more
than the darkness I live in
with my armor on…

~ *Young Stallion* ~

All Sales Are Final

❧

My attitude about my situation,
it strikes some as weird.
After all, I'm serving life
and have done so now going on fifteen years.
"Don't you ever want to get out?" they ask.
"What about all you are missing;
all life's niceties–
surely there is something in the free world you miss–
a decent meal; a relationship;
the choices not found in prison?"
And I can only smile my self-conscious grin,
and wonder if my eyes look opaque.
Sometimes I try to explain my thinking;
that this is my life
the one I bought, and am paying for.
But it doesn't register, so instead I say;
all sales are final, and
leave it at that.

~ Patrick Nolan ~

And the Light Shineth in Darkness

❧

Fluorescent candles
burn with sterile opulence
into the night:

Bleached tentacles
clinically assess
the contours of my
confinement

I sit in judgment;
looking to shadows
for comfort, turning
this way and that...

there is no escape
from the
glare
that renders nakedness.

~ Patrick Nolan ~

In this Savannah

❧

A black lion, much nobler
than a panther
with his thick mane turning gray,
languishes in the cool shade of a canopied tree,
ferocious to the eye
of would-be lion kings.

In the Savannah,
this lion king's domain,
a distant danger draws inward,
great beasts become extinct,
caught in a noose of constricting horizons.

He knows too
the time is near –
when his throne will be over-thrown
by those less noble, without respect.

A time will come
when the kingdom becomes
a desolate terrain filled
with jackals and vultures.

~ Patrick Nolan ~

The Soul Protector

❧

That soul shaking experience took place in May of this millennium year. I was trying to understand the meaning of man and learn how to face my fears. I closed my eyes to focus and saw my Inner Child in tears, and I knew at that moment that parts of my soul needed to die so my Inner Child could see clear.

I never could understand that I was the gardener of my own soul, and everything that I planted was destined to grow. I sacrificed my life to allow my mighty protector to show,
and in doing so my garden became a place that I learned to go…

On May 23 I knew it was time for my Inner Battle to begin. I faced off against rage and pain while I tracked a spirit full of sin. That unloving demon had betrayed me by convincing me it was my friend, so I stalked the betrayal that he portrayed and vowed to kill him in the end…

On May 24 a full blown war was staring me in the face. I prepared myself for death as my heart began to race. I knew something was gonna die and in my soul that death did take place, and in the moment of my rebirth I realized peace and love can fill a lot of empty space…

Dedicated to all my warrior brothers
That helped me to understand the meaning
Of a Warrior Man…

~ Soul Protector ~

Untitled Number Ten

He wanted more for us
Than what we have
And what we have is hate
What inspires us is fear
And the fear we hate
Silently eats away at who we are
And who we are disgusted us enough
To try the medicine of the Circle.

~ Healing Wolf ~

Listening to I

❧

Have a look, slow down your parade; time is going nowhere.
Only us, buried alive, can feel our organs consuming
themselves…calling to us to stop them.
But, our body is only too happy to oblige.
Don't ask yourself why—Yes!
It is a cruel & painful reality, a rude awakening—
but do you prefer to keep living in blind silence?
And ignore all the lives you've helped destroy?
To walk around imitating a life, knowing you're decaying inside?
Don't you see, we are now even near to be the men
we hope to become.
Society—
Our Society, doesn't count us among the living.
We only exist in their stored data
buried deep in bowels of some computer chip,
like all those dearly departed we are but just a fading memory.
Don't you realize!
Your funeral was held at the courthouse when you were sentenced.
You were there, your lawyer was there, the judge & DA.
And maybe some of your loved ones.
They were all there to see you go,
to witness your grand act of disappearing.
That was only part of the end now, it's up to you
to start living (to come out of darkness)
Maybe, time will give you another chance to become once more
a living creature, a capitalized name amidst your desired destiny.
Are you going to be the same?
You know…that one—that put you away in hell?
Or are you going to start becoming what you were meant to be?
Your echoes in here might be only a dying noise
but maybe—in the living world
they'll be a song many would want to hear.

~ Fierce Fox ~

Lies

I'm innocent.

I don't belong here.

If they let me out of here today

I'd never break another law.

I've learned my lesson.

I'm sorry for what I did.

I never said I was perfect.

I don't know why I do what I do.

I never meant to hurt anyone.

I'm not a bad guy.

I'll change.

~ Passionate Warrior ~

Gloom

☙

Gloomy days of unfulfilled boredom.

Looking for distractions from feeling.

A purpose to make it through the attitude.

Hoping beyond hope, that meaning isn't lost.

Exploring the unfamiliar.

Desperate without guidance,

Grasping to tickle joy out of life.

~ Healing Wolf ~

Silent

❧

Do you remember the old question? "If a tree was to fall in the forest
and nobody was around, would it make a sound?"
Would it's roots being ripped from the earth, remain silent?
Would it's crashing through the canopy of the forest not whisper a single
word?
Would it's massive trunk slamming to the ground not try with it's last
breath to cry out in pain?
Would not the other trees weep in sorrow for the loss of their brother?
The answer is yes, one only need listen.
Do you remember the old question?
If you lock a man in prison and he screams, would he make sound?
I can say I have screamed for ten years in silence, not a single head was
turned, not one ear was given.
Does not my voice carry the weight of a man?
If I lifted my hand to help you, would it not feel the same as yours?
If I gave my food to nourish you, would your body not grow?
If I covered you with my blanket when you were cold, would your
bones still shiver?
If someone wished to hurt you and I stood in your place, would my pain
be any less?
If I reached out to love you, would the gift be any less sweet?
The answer is yes, one only needs to care!
Then I met a group of men, and their name became:
"Inside Circle"

There is a man in this circle, Lion that Sometime Chatches Fire, who
in his own way put his arm around me and said; "I hear your screams, I
understand, and I love you for it." Man! That has changed my life and I
love you Rob!

~ Indio ~

Broken

≈

If your not broken, if your perfect and can find no flaws in yourself that you need to address, why the hell are you sitting in this room?

Look around you, look long and hard at the men who brave enough to crawl bloody and broken from a life of pain, sorrow, and sadness.

See me my perfect brother? I am broken I am not perfect and I will never be. I have many and I do mean many flaws I need to address.

That's why I sit in this circle today and that's why I will be sitting here next week and next year and for the rest of my life.

In looking at my brokenness I found my goodness, I found my compassion, I found my hope.

It was given to me by men who are broken and flawed and still brave enough to address it without having to fix it. It was a gift from men who understand, broken and flawed men who long to be loved...

~ Painted King ~

Why Complain if All Sales Are Final?

Opening my eyes to receive the new day, it doesn't take me long to be greeted by the same old reality-that I'm still in prison.

What's going to be today - who's going to fall - what new drama will be unfolded? Thinking of the day ahead, I utter my daily prayer "Holy Creator give me the strength to survive another day."

Breakfast will be here soon, I can already feel a nagging complaint forming up in my brain…No! Today, I'm going to break the norm. I will not start the day with complaints of how bad the food & life in prison is.

I know of others-in other parts of the planet who have it worse than I do, and unlike me, all they did to deserve their ill-fate was to have been born. So, why should I give into this absurdity of self pity?

Going deep within I start to see the endless parade of excuses. I unconsciously have accumulated through-out all these years of thinking of my self-the-victim and not those whom I've directly or indirectly hurt.

When this frightening realization starts to sink deeper, I can't help but wonder about the countless souls suffering under brutal regimes, dying of hunger-dying of AIDS-kids being sold as cheap as a commodity, sometimes even by their own parents. Who hears these unfortunate creatures' cries? What merciful savior will come down to heal their wounds?

Sure, I am without my freedom, but at least at the end of the day, I still have a choice. No, today I refuse to complain. It seems to me that I've been complaining for no good reason other than I can. I get three meals a day, two hot ones and one in a paper sack. I have a roof over my head, clean clothes, a bed to sleep on, a TV and radio to keep me entertained–not to mention the love and loyalty of my family, and some good friends. So, there's no reason to start the day with a brand new complaint. What gives me the right to rage about the way I'm being treated, or the endless lockdowns I have to endure? Especially when, I did commit a senseless crime.

Some people believe that maturity comes with old age. I however believe maturity is found in taking responsibility of our actions, whether they're right or wrong.

A good friend of mine once wrote: "all sales are final." When I first read this, I didn't (nor did I care to) understand what he was trying to convey. However, it's clear to me now what that bold statement means. You see, my friend took another's life, and it got him a long stay (in prison). So, since he took a life, he felt that he owed a life "his," therefore he was here to stay, without any complaints.

~ Fierce Fox ~

Foot Races of the Soul

⌖

As I sleep my soul journeys in no particular direction,
drifting by distant memories of sweet smells and fading
laughter...And then without warning my soul turns and
begins to run through twisted, burning steel and endless
miles of concrete. Like a tomb which there is no escape.
Suddenly I'm awake, dripping with fear; the foot race
has begun again as it has everyday, year after year. A
journey of indescribable pain and horror...
Although my body may seem still with no signs of movement
my barefooted soul runs it's race trying to out run all emotions...
Emotions are like an evil, foul smelling toothless beast,
and with him travels loneliness, despair, hatred, anger,
hopelessness and suicide...
And so my soul runs...trying to stay one step ahead of
the nightmare that follows, if my soul runs fast enough
I can keep the monstrous beast from catching up with me all at once...
My soul runs...sometimes a little piece of loneliness
will kick me, my soul runs, and a chunk of hatred will be
waiting for me around the corner. My soul runs, suddenly
a slice of despair and a crumb of hopelessness slap me
across the face...My soul runs...
When I finally come to an open field, sunny and bright,
and a soft breeze is blowing, the smell of flowers are
thick in the air...It is a break in the madness and for
a moment my soul rests...
But like a pack of wolves, my emotions stalk me from
the edge of my mind, always thinking...
The smell of rotten flesh is upon me and I realize I'm
being eaten and torn apart. The wolves have tracked me
down like a wounded deer in the snow...
I scream for my life! Knowing that all my emotions are
squeezing my throat, choking the life from my body. Suicide

is not far away now…I break free, my soul runs…
When I look upon the many distorted faces of the men
whom share my tragedy, I look for the signs. Like shadows in
the corner of my eye I can see their souls running a foot
race against unseen demons…
And when I listen real close I can hear the naked feet of
the souls, slapping on the concrete as they run past…
I run the edge of insanity now, and like some old ancient
form of torture I feel my body breaking and growing old
with time…
Now the bones in my feet are broken, and my flesh is torn
but still my soul runs.

~ Indio ~

If I Was to Bare My Soul

~

If I was to bare my soul to the world, surely the world would turn on me. If I were to once more become the innocent child I once was before time and life imposed it's fucked up expectations, peer pressure, prison rules, and the "hate what you don't understand" concept, how would I feel?

I'm forced to live on the razor's edge where every act and move must be well thought out before execution. If I were to dance with joy, the razor would destroy me. If I stomp too hard, or move too fast, I get cut...

I'm one of the lucky one's. I have found a place where I can bare my soul to my brothers without them turning on me. In this place my pain is welcomed and they understand it. They feel it, they all know my pain on an intimate level and are stronger because of it.

In this place the innocent child I once was, runs free. Without expectations, peer pressure, prison rules don't apply at all in this world and "hate what you don't understand" has no chance in hell here. In here it's RAW, it's real. I'm not only allowed to be me, but it's demanded. How could I be anything but me, when only the truth is spoken? These men everyone of them, are an asset to the world, and the world is so fucked up it threw us away. Now we heal and love each other.

I sometimes have this profound thought that maybe crime does pay.

~ *Painted King* ~

Sour Love

❧

Don't seduce me with that Elder love that protects me from myself.

That kind of love is the silk spider's web that wraps around me and strangles my growth.

Use that love instead to strengthen the container where I can smash the images and shields I created to hide behind.

Use that love to nurture the fragile part of me I rediscover after being broken open.

Don't let your love turn into fear that I can't handle the truth, so you shield me from my shadows.

Give me your love in the powerful strength of compassionate understanding from smashing your own images and shields instead.

~ Healing Wolf ~

The Five Steps of Finding "It"

&

Something brought you here, what were you hoping to find?

(1) What are you doing to find "it?"

(2) What committed are you to finding "it?"

(3) How committed are you to finding "it?"

(4) What keeps you from finding "it?"

(5) What will you do with it if and when you find "it?"

After more than four years that's what it's still about for me, just finding "it." What I know for sure, "it" changes with time.

For me at first, "it" was just a place to relax and be safe being me. That's all I hoped to find. Then when I found that, I realized that wasn't what it was for me at all. At that point it turned into needing to remember how to cry or at least remember when the last time I cried was. It came as a huge shock that I couldn't remember the last time I cried, or for that matter I was not even sure I could cry anymore. Keep in mind that at this point in my life I was still playing the tough guy shit. So being a hard ass patch wearing, race hating, convicted killer, not knowing how to cry should of raised me up a notch or two on the old bad ass meter. But that isn't what happened at all; it made me decide right then and there, that I was gonna remember how to cry. So "it" became the ability to cry, and I went to work.

After six months of sitting on my ass just watching stronger men than me do their work, I kind of had a clue that this could get real ugly and "it" wasn't gonna happen unless I did what I had to do...I had to stop hiding and step up. So if I wanted to find the elusive "it," "I pass," was no longer an option

Lucky for me there was some real high powered men there who were willing to help me. There was Manny, Smiley, Steve, TP, Antwon, Smoky, Rob, Dennis and many more. Watching these guys I learned to work. I've seen truth and integrity, fear, sadness, anger and shame. I've even seen joy and I started to remember how to feel.

I got into "it," and "it" became a drug to me. "It" wasn't knowing how to cry, "it" was knowing how to feel and how to live and love. Now "it" is teaching others. "It" always changes for me. In teaching others, I teach myself how to love them and how to love myself without expectations or judgments. So "it" becomes acceptance and forgiveness…"It" right now to me is Spirit or God or what-ever name you need to put on "it." "It's" a light inside me and you and every living thing that ever was or ever will be. "It" is life changing, "it" is the power that can take a cold blooded convicted killer and turn him into a man who wants to bring love to the un-loved. "It" is the only thing worth finding…I'll spend the rest of my life finding "it," and I will spend the rest of my life living with "it."…

~ Painted King ~

235

Blessed

～

Blessed with the honor to serve another man's pain

I bow to his lead of torment

Bravely speaking his truth

His heart drips slowly and laments

Speed escalating into a ferocious rage

Boiling point quickly met

Venomous poison spent is well earned

Providing relief for his tormented brave heart

Royal accomplishment of crowning deed

Purified feelings of his courageous act

Spirit has fed the Circle again.

~ Healing Wolf ~

Truth

My poison
Is no longer strong enough to kill me
From this day forward
I will take responsibility for my actions
No one has the power to fix me or change me
Only the power to guide me on the path I've chosen
Knowledge from my Elders
Is given to me in love, compassion & respect
For the courage I've shown to face my past and present
My wounds will never heal all the way
But with work done in this Circle
I will never let them bleed me dry
I've learned to think as a man
I will not allow the ghost of yesterday to haunt me
I've been given healthy weapons
To battle my demons to surrender their hold on my soul
I will fight them on my terms
Not theirs
I will never try to drown out their cry's again
I've also learned
That I have medicine to give fellow travelers
On an endless road.

~ Loving Leopard ~

Dear Anger

❧

Dear anger,

I am glad for your presence at times, somehow even in the madness and pain, I manage to see beyond a warriors armor and know that it is the only tool at hand to do the task at hand. The task at hand? To let out enough energy from that emotional cemetery where I bury what I don't want to feel, so that there's room for that undercurrent that's driving him or I to hide under something.

Anger, I do not understand your properties, your ability to magnify and disguise true emotions, you are a strange one indeed. One ounce of sadness can be a ton of mad in your hands, the symbolic albatross around my neck.

Sometimes, I revel in your horrific bliss and enjoy the cascade of power that I feel course through me making me a god. Sometimes I want to hang my head in shame and stop speaking; that allowed you to hold sway over me with something so small.

I see the magnificence of shining armor you can create around other warriors, each bearing the same exact message "don't fuck with me." At times I see you for what you are, a shadow, a defense, a condition, sometimes you are my savior. But not today. I see you as you are; a tool. A tool I will now use to carve a new armor out of, a transparent armor, thin as a gossamer of silk and lacking the ability to stop any weapon yet possessing the quality of spider silk it will ensnare them and trap them so I can view them at my leisure, so I can better understand them and in turn use them to my benefit.

Anger, you are no longer the king of the tribe of I. You are usurped and dethroned, not yet exiled as you have your use and your day and time. I know from time to time you will plan your insurgencies and revolts but you will fail because I see you as you are. A tool and I will use you to carve a new armor transparent and thin as a gossamer of silk, no longer repelling but now ensnaring. I am king and I assert my birthright.
Sincerely Your King

~ *King Mongoose* ~

I Do It Afraid

~

What proves I haven't given up on myself is:

I Do It Afraid.

What I'd been doing unafraid doesn't work.

My choice is to say: "Fuck – it"

Even when I'm afraid,

I ask for what I want,

Keeping it real.

~ Healing Wolf ~

I Didin't Like'Em Then

❧

When I first saw'em walk,
With a powerful stroll,
That warned of danger,
Yeah, I didn't like'em then.

The way he bragged about bullying,
Or his leer about pressuring,
And his laugh at others weakness'
Oh, and the blood lust about his victims,
Yeah, I didn't like'em then.

Guys I liked, even my friends,
Said he was a good dude…
I really wondered about that,
I really wondered about them.
Couldn't they see what I saw?
I didn't like'em then either.

Once I watched him tell his drag,
How he worked his female friend.
She gave her heart to'em, he kept his.
Yeah, I didn't like'em then.

As I write this,
In my head I turn the page
And to my embarrassed surprised,
I've done all this shit too.
Yeah, I didn't like me then either.

~ Healing Wolf ~

My Mother's Fingers

❧

My mother's fingers were long
like mine, and whatever she touched
took on a life all its own:
lines on canvas
soon became a caress
from which flowers
flourished; red glistening
tulips., dewy blue-violet irises
asleep in the midmorning
sun, pink roses on rich
green vines: each thorn
a large ripe grape.
Once as a child
I watched those same
fingers nurse the wing
of a young Monarch
butterfly:
there was an understanding
in such tenderness that haunts
me today when I wash my face,
passing scarred fingers over
grayIng eyes.

~ *Patrick Nolan* ~

August – Month Eight

MEMORIES, DREAMS, LOSS, LOVE

Frozen thoughts become memories, remembered wrongly and they often invade our night time terrain tormenting us as dreams. The book of memories opens to the chapter of "should have done."

Other memories are imprisoned like photographs. Messages from the past churn fragmented pieces of memories. In the dusty hallways of our minds, through the doorways of our past, favorite memories protect us against pain and uncertainty. Odd happenings can spark a memory and instantly transport one to the sad child inside the adult who then created ugly hateful memories. Feelings can be put on hold, to match them with old memories. Nightmares speak in the language of images, not of words, and can't see it when I'm looking right at it.

There's a woman that'll save me from myself and my indescribable and insatiable needs. Often there's a hunger for nasty love even if it'll rip us apart. The fear of exposing the heart, often carries a lifetime of unspoken words and emotions and tortured love.

Cold violent love can leave one with macabre thoughts and huge distances between killing for love or because of love. Love can pierce feeling-proof-armor, conspiring in it's delights. The dark side of love can keep us in fear and rage. Reading about someone else's loss of love, doesn't tell me how to lose my own love either.

Untitled Number Three

✍

My porcelain beauty
Do visions of me plague your thoughts?
Do I now define your existence?
Many questions come to mind and I ask,
do I kindle your passion?
Your desires to be free?
To love to feel?
Let me break through your caged heart & free your soul.
Let me fly into the depths of your being and seek what I know to be
true.
Am I closer to your completion?
Do I fill your need?
If not let me satisfy your every curiosity.
I want to swim in your veins,
crawl under your skin,
flushed & steadily pumped into your heart stream.
I only ask because I am lost within your love.
And should I do none of these things,
let me know now,
so I can kill this love inside of me
before it takes a life of it's own.
Love is reborn & I cannot stop its birth.
I implore you,
should I let it continue to grow or deny it right to live?
I know no other phenomenon other than Life or death,
but love is extraordinary because it can bring both forth,
both pleasure and pain.

~ Dancing Cobra ~

Remember

❧

Stay now, now that earth spins ashes at the stars...

It is morning and I creep awake into an anxious silence that was once for prayers. The year is gone, crossroads the good year of a green and deathless spring, a summers toil. In Autumn it rained, and just now the morning sun attempts to find me through dirty glass and stretch along a grey faceless wall. I would send back the day for a moment more of the prayerless dark if I could.

But stay now, now that the earth spins ashes at the stars and remember the poets who sat among the potshards and broken totems of their tribes wrapping grief in tongues, who sat upon the hearths, upon the severed marble heads, songs resounding of silent tels turning our lives to myth, the scroll of everyday unwinding tomorrow with each broken seal. Stay now, maybe one last time, like dry seeds in expectant earth.

Somewhere there are bricks laid by immigrants into the walls of an alley where sometime poets slept between Mad Dog and matins, saxaphone prayers in halfstep caught in a century of mortar while streets turned grey, while Bird and Coletrane turned to myth while buses went to Chicago while none stood at the.........with a price on their souls, no more seller's remorse in all the bent and dragging notes that masked the flaws that make beautiful our cry.

But stay now and remember the scarecrows heaped in Auschwitz trenches;remember the guided cry of temple horns on the morn before Christ died. Remember the sprinkled laugh of children before the infamy of age, the eternity that lingers before the touch of lover,s lips. Remember most musicians fade unheard, most poets lie buried under piles of dead, pressed trees, that hope is tenacious curiosity in what the world will be flaming blue ball of smoky glass spinning ashes at the stars maybe one last time.

So stay now

~ Shaman's Key ~

On the Porch

❧

My soul walks the old pathways of my lives in bliss recounting lost loves. Memories faded from the harsh light of living, twisting and turning like creeper vines flipping their best side up to receive the breath of the sun. I stop on a memory and wait; it feels good here. I step into the moment. I revel in the newly awakened time of my life. Familiarity seeps into my being; I spent much time here comfortable, I relax and feel. Wax from mosquito candles, lilacs in a basket, newly clipped grass, the waft of oil and grease on concrete, old spice, and sugar cookies. Cicidas sing the lonely hymn, the chirp of sparrows nesting in the eaves, the creak of lawn chair plastic on flesh, the hum of a passing car on a corner, the buzz of streetlights, and melting ice clinking in a glass on its way to oblivion. Bats darting through the trees chasing moonlight, lightning bugs dancing and firing their salvos of love, the glow on the side of my grandfather's face in the light from the house, and my grandmother rocking in her chair and the feeling of being wanted and loved.

~ King Mongoose ~

Restless Wonder

❧

Unable to get a night's sleep
I lay awake, letting my mind go wild
awaiting the next day...
A drop of hope rushes through.
Never understanding the riddle–my life is...
All seems pointless.
Not having a reasonable meaning
not giving me a moment of rest.
I drift through the night
filled with desperate thoughts
awaiting that moment of rest,
not finding refuge in fantasies.
My mind feeds on thoughts
old memories.
How miserable it is
to remember the joy
I once had.
Now those memories
only pound the cruel reality
of what
has become my life...

~ Fierce Fox ~

Raven

❧

Black wings, black wings,
Beating late in the night.
Flickering flame, fire light.
Red eyed Raven on his perch,
Staring through the window,
Pretending he's not there,
Gripped in fear,
Head on my pillow.
Tap, Tap, Tap,
Crooked beak against the glass.
From under my covers
I can hear his twisted laugh.
Squawk, Squawk,
Raven spits his ugly spell.
Stumbling from bed,
I tremble in the corner of my cell.
Come and dance with me, he says,
Hold my dirty black wing,
Wrap it around your neck, from the roof,
Use that old boot string.
I thought about it for a moment,
His offer I almost took.
But when I went to jump from the toilet,
My body only shook.
Feathers, flesh, blood and bone,
Within that face is where he hides.
I've seen him dance,
I've seen him fly,
He goes by the name of, SUICIDE!!!

~ Indio ~

I'm Going to Be a Poet

❧

I'm going to be a poet
and people will whisper as I walk by,
"See that Guy? He's a poet."
And I'm going to be a good poet,
they get laid more.
I want people to read what I write
and remember it forever.
Remember to cry,
and to heal,
and to riot,
and to rise.
I'll let my hair grow
because poets can.
I won't work,
not nine to five,
good poets don't.
My hands will be rough
from cutting wood
and my skin brown
from being outdoors.
And I'll fish and write
and hike and read
and with words.
I'll speak and listen
as poets do.
Yes, I'm going to be a poet.

~ Passionate Warrior ~

Cliff Dweller

❧

As a child I raced among these notches in rock. Up and down the ladders chasing and being chased laughter ahead and behind me triumphing my arrival and marking my territory. Now no one is here. I climb a ladder and look inside the room, I see invisible things come back to haunt me. I feel a sense of loss and shame. I left here so long ago and this place was so full of life, where are the smells that hung in the air? The low hum of life that was always present is no longer. I stare at the huge wide ladder that leads up to the rooms of my childhood. The rungs oversized and still too large for my now mannish hands. How did I climb these rungs before to receive my training, my rewards, my punishments? The journey up this ladder sometimes an instant, sometimes an eternity. I start up the ladder to stop, I step back down into the dust and face outward looking across the plain before me, I decide that any room I will see is empty. I just look out across the plain from my ledge and I stand in the setting suns staining light and just feel. I feel a sense of loss and shame.

~ King Mongoose ~

Unknown

❧

Broken bones scattered in the road,
some are mine,
some are yours.
The roof is gone,
the walls splattered with blood.

Worms feasting in the flesh
swarming all around me
but yet I eat this heart.

The sun is gone.
Darkness has arrived.
I dream of you again.

~ Grim Reaper ~

Bad Girl Only Girl

☞

It seems I have always had to have a bad girl, there just ain't no room for nice girls in my world. I like them nasty.

I need one that speaks from the heart. Even if what she has to say may rip me apart.

They've got to be real.
Save the games and all the weak yuppie drag; life's a horse race and I won't be riding a nag.

I need her tenderness. I need a women who never gives up. She has to be a baby tiger, not some weak little pup.

I'm not saying she must hide her tears, I'm only saying she has to be strong enough to face her fears.

Win or lose it doesn't matter to me. If she is real I will be there for eternity. I will live and die for her if only she tries. It's over as soon as she lies.
I only want one bad girl but I want one that wants me more than anything else in the world.

~ Painted King ~

My Devoted Love

~

My devotion stands like a madman in love
deliriously laughing, proclaiming my undying affection.
Heaven and earth have heard,
and so shall you on this momentous occasion.
For on this day
the stars shall night will be my eyes;
Picturing wrapped in satin laced sheets;
Redefining your sensuous curves.
A winged bird will be my messenger.
Sending you these words
I have conspired for all of your delightments.
My desire to be near you is transparently clear;
inspired by your love, patience and due diligence.
This is my dedication to you.
Time has no more meaning and together;
Forever is a real concept.
And this day shall be forged in time,
As yours and Mine.

~ Dancing Cobra ~

Man in the Glass

～

When I look at the man in the glass,
I see the scars of his bloody past.
The carefree smile he had that the girls loved so,
Has been replaced with an evil sneer.
His young skin has been covered with tattoos
Of skulls, bars, and demons.
When I look at the man in the glass,
I don't see the man I knew in the past,
I don't see the man who use to wake up his son so they could play,
I can no longer see him laugh or roll in the grass with his dog.
He no longer wakes up every morning loving life.
When I look at the man in the glass,
I wonder what ever happened to my past…

~ *Painted King* ~

Unknown

❧

O…LONELINESS…WHY…
DO YOU…TORMENT ME
WHY CAN'T YOU…
JUST…LEAVE ME BE
YES…I FEEL…
THE EMPTINESS…DEEP WITHIN
AS…I LONG TO…
EXPERIENCE LOVE…AGAIN
AS…I NEED TO FEEL…
THAT…POWERFUL BOND…
THAT…LEAVES ME FEELING…
SO FAR…BEYOND
THE DEEPENING SENSE…
OF BEING ALONE
LEFT…TO WALK THROUGH…
LIFE…ON MY OWN
I DO NOT LIKE…
FEELING…THIS WAY
JUST DRIFTING THROUGH…
EACH…AND EVERY DAY
BUT…ONE DAY…
YOU'RE SURE…TO BE GONE
AND FEELINGS…OF LOVE…
CAN BEGIN…TO DAWN!!!!

~ Unknown ~

My Forgotten History

❧

Signs of our past are everywhere-old monuments…
that once stood, as symbols of might are now mere reminders
of a vanishing culture…
In those old days thousands marched to be slaughtered
to pacify the hunger of ancients gods…
Until the new rulers came;
they brought their understanding and corruption's of the new world;
gold was their mistress disguised as their God…shrouded with holy
words
spoken by this Jesus they seemed to love, and hate so much.
No one really knows what went on in those days-
History…has been twisted, and composed by way too many pens.
I say to hell with history, and its many roads of false understandings.
I can't hate
those that criticize the ones who killed
for the life giving light of their creators…
-I AM MESTIZO-
A living testament
of that chapter
in our world…
I am a citizen of Earth-
and I declare this to be
My Truth.

~ *Fierce Fox* ~

A Night in LA

~

The loud gunshots echoed waking-up the slumberous neighborhood,
A fast moving car burned wheels from the source of the sound.
Family and friends held each other and cried where they stood,
As they prayed for the boy that was bleeding to death on the ground.
It didn't take long for the street to fill to some kind of order.
For some reason most had tears of sadness even the working hookers,
Then blocking the crime scene with tape, the officers made a border.
The approaching ambulance came a little to late,
Because the bleeding boy closed his eyes and met his fate.

~ Turtle ~

Unknown

❧

Holding the picture in my calloused hand
I dwelled on the many
captured in just this one.
It was a collage
covered with photos
of my life.

In their eyes
and facial expressions
they hold the same old burdens
that still curse me;
they are all me, the man I have become.
There is no solace
in the empty eyes staring back at me.
They don't give me the understanding
that I desperately seek.
Only a troubled past
of a life I wish
I had never
had to live.

~ Silver Wolf that Cares for the Pack ~

Untitled Number Five

You can't see
that I could be one
that you might love

or one that
might kill you

or one you
might kill

or kill for.

~ Shaman's Key ~

Credo?

❧

I sound interior
skies for sight of self;
a slow waking delirium;
disequilibrium
panic
vertigo
amnesia–more a dissipating
disembodiment
from
feeling emotions
from
visceral memories

where have I been
throughout this maelstrom
of oblivion wherein the fragmented
pieces of my being churn.

I look at the moon in my memories,
mercurial pool
cold and distant, enclosed in the dark plethora of my heart.

~ *Patrick Nolan* ~

Truth is Inverted Pain

⌒

I watched a man
quickly deteriorate
far from his family
wrapped in the quiet
comfort of tomhill suburbia.

Six miles away
from his family
he sat on the splintered wooden
steps of a back alley flat waiting
waiting thin elbows on thin knees,
and he would wave to me as I passed
him by, and I would wave back not
thinking to mention having seen his
two sons–school mates – the day
before who knew only that their
father one day, suddenly went away, gone forever from their lives,
from those rickety splintered steps
until I realized, ten years later writing
a poem to a friend I never said good-bye.

~ Patrick Nolan ~

A Love Poem

๛

A beauty to die for,
an innocence to kill.
A love of infinite possibilities
from which I hide.
Intimate words
and tender kisses
crumble my walls.
Exposing my nakedness,
from which I hide.

~ Passionate Warrior ~

My Father's Words

❧

As I sat at his table, I watched my father eat.
With the wide eyed wonder of a little boy,
I watched his every move, and listened,
for the words that never came.
Nothing ever said.
But all words understood.
Milk, gravy and biscuits, along with pork chops,
and a glass of buttermilk.
I watch my father eat, silent.
I hung on his every move.
I searched his face for the stern look, that said to me,
that I was part of him, and he was part of me.
Then when he passed the bowl of gravy to me,
somehow it all become so clear.
All that he ever wanted to say to his son,
but couldn't, was all in that bowl of gravy.
The passing of food to his son, was his way of saying, I love you.
That bowl of gravy carried the weight of an entire lifetime of unspoken
words, and hugs and pats on the back, and kisses,
and tears, and laughter and stories, and lessons.
That bowl of gravy said so much to me
when I was a little boy, that even today
I can feel it's weight in my hands.
Nothing was ever said that day at the table,
but my ears still ring
with my fathers words.
Now I still try and listen for my father's voice
which is so hard to find even in our old age.
If only he would pass that bowl of gravy to me,
just one more time.
That day at the table
we were father and son.
So much like humans, acting like wolves.

~ Indio ~

Upon a Sparrow Wing

☞

I took a walk again last night, down that long dark hallway full of doors with shiny knobs. In the darkest times of my life when I no longer want to keep on going, and death seems as sweet as a woman's tender kiss. I walk down this dusty hallway that lives in my mind, and I open these doors one-by-one that lead me to the places and faces of the past.

That is the place where I still live, where I still smile and laugh, where I still dance in the arms of loved ones. But it is also the place where nightmares are born. There is one door at the very end of this hallway that I open the most and I open it so much that dust never collects there. Its knob has been turned so many times, that it has become worn and smooth like glass. Behind this door she's always standing, holding our daughter. And I see in her eyes that she loves me and is glad that I have returned to open the door once again.

But last night was different. When the knob was turned and the door was opened she was no longer standing there. Instead I seen myself lying face down in a giant sea and I was dead. I had finally drowned myself in the deep - icy waters of her memory. I watched myself floating in her sea of blue waters when a dolphin swam up to my body and began to swim circles around me. Slowly pushing me to the shore as he sang to me in the language of Lost Souls. He pushed me upon the beach, and with a final melody from his song, disappeared beneath the waters. For what seemed like an eternity, but was only a short time, I watched my body lying there on the beach as the waves of her memory licked at my body. And tiny crabs began to feast upon my flesh. When out of the sky–a sparrow did fly. And landed where my body now lies. With his little beak he pulled a single strand of hair from my head, back upon his wing, towards the mountains I was lead. There on a mountain the sparrow dug a tiny hole, and buried my single strand of hair. That hair grew into a giant tree, and I now see that tree is me, forever is lost my body to her sea.

So now I live on this mountain; her memory and smile I will forever sing.

My love for her flies upon a sparrows wing.

~ Indio ~

Sorrowful Night

❧

Dark night of sorrow, hold your arms above the stars, so I may
see your majestic view.
Look upon your creation and see your work of darkly thoughts,
lovers in scorn, plotting devilish schemes.
And in the midnight hour tempers rage and lovers are dead upon
their stage.
And in the next scene of things;
tortured Love comes from fling.
And there a boy of seventeen plunges into his last remaining
dream. Care to see hopelessness? Yes. Hope no less.
Sweet little girl turned out to the world, player her last dare
at Russian roulette.
So suffer me no more for I have seen your careless hands.
Naked baby boy born with epileptic seizures and yet he
understands.

~ Dancing Cobra ~

Love

ॐ

Love…Love is not the sun of springtime joy
Nor the light of morning air that kisses the lips of some voluptuous
woman.
It is neither a rose that blooms in some unkept garden.
(Who say Love is this?) must be eligible for an asylum for he can not be
sane.
Mad he is, for show me a love none full of secrets;
and secrets has its prize.
But what prize is worthy of celebration if love secrets hide from thee?
No. Love is cold and violent.
Winters fiercest fray.
Take that rose and its prick of thorns
prick like cupids arrow, and see its scorn darts its way,
christening your softly padded palms.
It has left men with macabre thoughts and driven madly towards suicide.
None the less,
yes. Love is pure.
Love spoken word is spoken in whispers for if aloud, it's heard, men's
souls would shatter.
So restrain and constrain your heart and refrain from Loves darkest
dominion.
And thou mayest be count thee blessed…, If love should be merciful
towards your death.

~ *Dancing Cobra* ~

The Letter

❧

A glimpse
a hope
a dream
something so fucking scary
it's all I can do
not to scream.

The one that can kill superman
faster than a room full of kryptonite;
the one thing that 's so fucking dangerous
it can make a meek monk willing to fight.

I got a letter in the mail
postmarked
the deepest depths of hell;
I opened it up
and pierced my
feeling-proof shell.

My mouth fell open
and I couldn't breathe anymore.
The contents rocked me
to my very core:

my wife sent me a letter
saying that she still
loves me.

~ Painted King ~

A Gerber Baby

The glass jar that once contained
baby food now held a hundred colored
buttons of various shapes & sizes.
I was ten then.
I remember how I'd fold and fluff the thick fabric
bed cover making tunnels and forts,
strategically placing button soldiers as I named each one.

My favorite was seashell shaped;
blue, not too big;
a keeper I carried in my pants pocket for protection
against the pain and uncertainty outside my imaginary play.

God!
To think I sat in bed for hours,
alone in a room I shared with my brother
and three sisters,
lost in a spell of make believe.

~ Patrick Nolan ~

Poetic Associations

Funny how a poem
can sweep you up,
transport you back to some forgotten
place in the past:

He lights a cigarette and, from habit, because he has always been poor,
counts those left in the package.
A Canadian poet's words; and,
although I no longer smoke,
I've lost count of all the times:
belly empty, ass cold, off to the side of the road,
hitching cross country;
I counted mine:

They took the edge
off hunger, made it bearable –
did I mention I no longer smoke,
or, that the highway led to prison and a life sentence in California?

I'm a Canadian too;
and last week a man died
from knife wounds to the heart –
I don't know if he smoked.

~ *Patrick Nolan* ~

Untitled Number Twenty One

*

Since I was a baby

My feelings were put on hold

Take a toke of this joint

See it's funny getting him high

Watch him devour that twinkie

His eyes are glassy

His pain is put out

~ Loving Leopard ~

A Beautiful Soul

How can such a beautiful soul
Devour my will to live

How can such a beautiful soul
Not care who it hurts

How can such a beautiful soul
Lie to me

How can such a beautiful soul
Not see me

How can such a beautiful soul
Discard my feelings

How can such a beautiful soul
Betray me

How can such a beautiful soul
Use me

How can such a beautiful soul
Throw me away

How can such a beautiful soul
Be black

Why'd I feel that I have to kill that beautiful soul
So I can stop hurting...

~ Loving Leopard ~

Lingering Lazy

～

Lingering lazily
in moments
of long ago

resting recklessly
in recaptured rapture.

Melting into
manufactured moments
of magnificence.

Stagnating in
sensuously
stimulating
stories

tempting to
tolerate time

truly tragic...

truly tragic...

~ Painted King ~

Loss

℘

Wounds that cut deep, deep into the soul
leaving gaping festering wounds that ooze
out sunshine and hope like a flood of blood.
Broken dreams bleed freely.
I refuse to dance around the meaning of my mission.
I'm going to use the word loss and I am not going to present it
in any other form than it's own.
So you endure the loss.
Write about loss they said,
Who's loss? Your loss? My loss? The loss
of men fighting to cling to something
more than insane screams?
Reaching and reaching daring to dream even in a place
where sadistic souls rip the wings off angels,
and then laugh at their demise.
I scream no more loss!!!! No more broken spirits.
No more nights planning and plotting ways to endure one more
needless loss.
Loss of hope is ripping out my soul.

Loss of compassion. Loss of what I want to be.
The Loss of me.
So tell me poet who's loss should I write about today?
Shall I write about the loss my victim's mother felt the day she found
out she lost her son?
Shall I write about the loss my mother felt the day she heard her son had
killed?
Shall I write about the loss my son feels over growing up without a dad?
Shall I write about the loss I felt as the cuffs bit into my tattooed skin?
Shall I write about the loss of sleep for years because of the loss?
Maybe I would give a better read if I wrote about
the years I thought my sanity would surely be my next and last loss.
I know loss and when I write about loss
I call it loss...

~ Painted King ~

Dennis

You knew me when I didn't care
and yet you were always there.

You knew me in my fear and rage
and yet you were always there.

My life has been transformed
I have touched the hand of God
and you were always there.

Now when I reach my hand out to others who don't care,
who fear or who are engulfed by their rage,
I find peace in knowing you are always there.

What you gave me
has no form no shape no color no sound.

Love is strange that way.
So where ever you may find your self
where ever God or your life may take you

I will always be there
in your heart
holding your hand
and watching you shine.

~ Painted King ~

September - Month Nine

RITUALS, INITIATIONS, TENACITY, HUNGER, CYCLES, STEPPING–OUT, CONFRONTING SELF, STOPS AND STARTS ON THE WAY TO REDEMPTION

Through the mysterious journey of life, one encounters many different obstacles. When one tenaciously seeks guidance, teachers or elders present themselves in response to the heart's call.

A special type of strength is required to endure the rituals of initiation. Seekers find unused paths, meet other souls and sacred beings in sacred space. Some seekers find obstacles that prevent them from accepting their waiting chair in the circle. Warnings are given by those who've been through the fire to those who hesitate.

Outer body experiences in search of our true selves lead to an awakening. Confrontations in anger can trigger an ability to change. Warless souls endanger friends in pursuit of the noble ideal of mystical healing offered by elders.

Holding one's sorrow caged in the sanctuary becomes an obstacle that won't let them out of themselves. It takes tenacity to keep facing fears on one's way to inner solace. If the seeker keeps on seeking, he must step out from behind the mask and become authentic. He must attempt again and again to unlock and free the little child inside, because he wants to be loved and be born into the dreams of life.

Unknown

❧

Again I have come to the point in a journey that was started? it was a travel that left me weary on the outside of my body, but thankfully renewed within! I shared in the various wells of men's poisons as well as their medicines; the rainbows were intoxication, sometimes to the point of suffocation, but there was always an antidote of love & beauty to revive me. I traveled with a stranger who trusted me to care for his heart & everything that he held dear and was fearful of, and that for me an invaluable gift itself, and we made a new beginning and created space for him to be able to take journeys to far away continents within, on that magic carpet! And so he can now travel with strangers with a special knowing that humanity is yearning for his gift that he now knows exists within himself, and can take those travels with others with wise footsteps.

Rob said at the start "that the men who dwelled here would be able to hold any container within the house." Well I know my hands are singed from the fire that was on my side of this house! Some unbelievable courage I sat with over there, and it made me feel – I come to help others feel and identify with the inner dragons, but couldn't stop the lava from coming to my volcano's spout – (Mike it happens to us all). I didn't personally get to see everyman's journey here, but I can honestly say I see it in every man's eyes and feel it in the spirit of this room! I can't begin to tell you the courage & strength I witnessed in this room, these men come from their balls and pulled out their swords of pureness to purge the earth of those poisons that have held them prisoner for so long and if nothing else I am a better man for sharing in these experiences!

You all honor me with your presence here and every man here is an honor unto the next and I hold that in my heart until my physical being leaves here!

Thank You All

~ *Wise Tiger* ~

The Circle

~

Wounds that cut deep, deep into the soul
leaving gaping festering wounds that ooze
out sunshine and hope like a flood of blood.
Broken dreams bleed freely.
I refuse to dance around the meaning of my mission.
I'm going to use the word loss and I am not going to present it
in any other form than it's own.
So you endure the loss.
Write about loss they said,
Who's loss? Your loss? My loss? The loss
of men fighting to cling to something
more than insane screams?
Reaching and reaching daring to dream even in a place
where sadistic souls rip the wings off angels,
and then laugh at their demise.
I scream no more loss!!!! No more broken spirits.
No more nights planning and plotting ways to endure one more
needless loss.
Loss of hope is ripping out my soul.

~ Passionate Warrior ~

Aho

She

They chanted as we gathered rolling thunder of the heart;
voices on the water that move the night apart;
and one by one we entered with our armor tightly drawn
and saw the elders standing along the road that we were on;
They sang Aho Aho!
I saw a battle-weary warrior with his shield down at his feet
cradle the fallen poet in the hour of his defeat
and I heard the roar of lions
and I saw the eyes of kings
and I heard the voice of truth rise up
like howling from the rings;
I heard Aho Aho!
And I who have no father
I who have no son
I whose way was twisted before the road begun
stood within the circle revealed by degrees
and when the veil was lifted
I went right down on my knees.
Do you know how it feels to have your life turn out as one big mistake?
(Aho)
Everything that you give don't ever quite balance out with the things
you take…
Do you know how it feels to be betrayed by the ones you loved and
trusted?
Do you know how that feels?
Do you know how that feels?
And they sang Aho Aho!
From the cold Bay O'Fundy to the gravel 'neath your feet;
from the potter's field of Georgia to broken islands of the Keyes;
may there be no unsung heroes, may the child sleep safe tonight,
may home find the wanderer and may all men find the light;
May they say Aho Aho.

~ Shaman's Key ~

Inner Strength

Inner strength reveals one's true worth.
It is in times of hardship that the test is
Passed or failed.

For who stands up in these times
Decides how you
Live you life.

When the world seems dark and cold
Can you find the strength to
Face the darkness
And outlast the cold?

At times such as these can you
Remember your
Inner strength and therefore
Remember your
True worth?

~ Painted King ~

Keeping It Real in the Gauntlet

If I keep it real
will my truth crush the will of the one I tell?
Will my truth hurt the feelings
of my circle brother so bad
that they can't handle it, they'll quit?

Where are the strong hearted warriors
that can brave the truths,
sit in the intense fires
that strengthen him or melt his armor
exposing what was hidden from view.

Truth can be unwelcomed
a load of crap
saying what's expected
instead of what they truly feel.

Where are the brave hearts
hungry to hear
the hearts of the sacred circle,
eager to face their poisons
unveil their shadows
challenge their fears
joyously battling again and again and again?

~ Healing Wolf ~

Alone, Empty and Unable To Cry

~

Alone with my thoughts,
half aware of sounds
filtering into my cell
under the steel door;
feeling lost, head pounding
as I try to make sense
of my emotions, turning
over stones for some
sort of answer, only
to find this slimy existence,
my life.
I think of a story
a parent might tell a child
when someone has died,
and I want to cry as I try
to imagine which star
is hers in the sky somewhere
above the gray weight
this cell's ceiling forbids
me to see, and all the old
cliches come barreling
down; what she meant to me;
how I will miss her;
and now this insatiable void
swallowing yet another
galaxy whole, and me a cold
asteroid filled with nothing
but nothing, hurling fast
and furious to nowhere,
unable to cry for that someone
I loved who has made the journey
over to the other side.

~ *Patrick Nolan* ~

Mountain in the Rain

Through the cold walls of gray
Through the faces of the un-retrieved
In his old black coat he makes his way
To the unremembered unredeemed

To those that pass, to the left behind
To those that linger in the promise of the light
To the hearts of glass, to the grieving mind
To the unsurrendered fatherless child

O man of God
You're like a mountain in the rain
O man of God
You're like a mountain in the rain

O man of God, did you see the light?
Did it fall like rain in the middle of the night?
Through spires of stones, from thorns and vines
Lord, did they call to drink this wine?

O man of God
You're like a mountain in the rain
O man of God
You're like a mountain in the rain

~ Shaman's Key ~

Kings

❧

It's 5:45 a.m. and I sit here on this steel toilet,

using the sparse light

shining through the dirty window in the steel door,

that's keeping me securely in my cement box.

As I reflect back over the last three days of my life,

a tear of joy streams down my face,

because for a second, a minute, an hour, a day,

a whole damn weekend

there was no doubt not one shred of doubt,

that I am walking with kings,

and that I'm a king and that you're a king.

And we have the power and the fire

to make all men who encounter us, kings.

We now know we are;

Wizards,
Lovers,
Warriors,
and we know each other as kings…

~ Painted King ~

Tough-Guy

~

So you think you're tough
and on your weakest day, down right rough.
The take no-shit kinda man, in for murder, robbery, and when you're
feeling nice, a little mayhem.
Yeah, don't think I don't see you, always looking hard,
constantly telling war stories, and how you can stroll any prison yard.
Well you can leave that shit at the door,
my friend, all your loudmouth ways and such.
Because to be honest with you partner, that kinda crap never has
impressed me much.
But if you really want respect,
and show what a big man you can be, then join the Inside Circle.
"Here" you can have the seat right next to me.
Seems pretty easy don't it? A candle, a carpet and a circle of men.
Then step up to the plate. We don't come here to pretend.
Don't tell me you're scared. Your knees are knocking, and your nerve is
rattled. You said you were a tough-guy, ready for any battle.
I'm not trying to pick on you, because it's not easy for any of us here.
But I can say this to you my friend. It takes a tough-man to shed a tear...
so let us sit and talk, and maybe even find,
the softer side of your nature, the real man,
the human "inside."
So come on tough-guy,
put your fears aside,
jump in the middle of the Circle.
Take that magic carpet ride.
Then when it's over
the mask is down & there is nowhere to hide.
After I've seen your wounds,
and you've witnessed mine,
that is the time, right there and then,
I'll be proud to call that
tough-guy my friend...

~ Indio ~

Kings

❧

So you want to sit in the fire.
You want to be the wounded pilgrim,
Durer's "Knight, Death and the Devil"
St. Anthony ripped by demons,
a Fisher King, a hermit, a hero.
So you want to break the mask
of your father, jump in the cauldron,
drown in the well, sit in sackcloth
and ashes scraping your disease
and boldly dare the dragon's den
to bathe in his burning blood.
So you want to show your wounds,
carry the cross, weep in the garden,
gasp in the whale's belly in hopes
he might puke you up somewhere…

So you want to sit in the fire.
Let those who have tell you,
let them tell you that mostly
it means getting your butt burned,
a mouthful of guts, of blood,
tears you prayed you'd never
have to cry and risking betrayal
when you hang naked. But let them
also tell you the world is waste
and the only gold there's ever been
has been in the fire.

~ Shaman's Key ~

Trash Heap

❧

Plucked from the deepest depths of a prison trash heap,
One of the forgotten and unloved.
Tossed aside by society
No longer allowed to participate in life
Beyond the razor wire and stone walls.

Gone from sight, given up on and most assuredly
Beyond any and all hope,
Tagged dubbed and numbered human waste nothing more.

After a decade in the prison trash heap,
A saint in state blues saved me.
He reached deep, past the trash
And grabbed what was left of me
And started the recycling process.

He placed me in a circle broken and dirty
Where I was washed clean with truth, honor, hope, and integrity.
Soon all the bloody trash of prison
Was washed away by the tears
Of my forgotten shame, sadness, fear, and joys.

I was forgotten no longer.
I became one of the truly loved.
I participated not only in my own self growth
But the growth of my convict brothers
Who had fell victim to the same lie that we were hopeless.
We debated that bald faced lie
And became great men of honor.
I now know no man is beyond hope,
If someone will love him enough,
To pluck him from the prison trash heap…

~ Painted King ~

September 12

Mystic Creatures

My spirit descends and I am left with an outer body experience, but I fear these words may betray my feelings.

The best I can come up with is that I'm left suspended in mid-air staring downward into dragon's lair.

Who slays monsters better than the Beastmaster, and can control the dragon better than the Dragon's Keeper?

I see the rabbits spirit swiftly moving through the dense forest and in the eternal sky, the Spirit Hawk soars and expands it's magnificent wings circling its sacred grounds. And there perched on its branch sit the Straight Eagle tall in its stature and beautiful in its nature.

And upon the cliff of Dead Man Falls howls the aging Grandfather Wolf with his shining white fur and gnarled teeth howling his pain so the dead can be remembered. What about the fruit fly that offers his nurturing; his insatiable lust for supplement; or the Bobcat with his brown coat and black spots moving ever so gracefully as a feline.

I am none of these things but a lone man desperately seeking my place in this vast and complex world.

I am walking through down the winding road searching for other selves. And in my 22 years of futile searching I have yet to find that man who not long ago was a little boy. Oh to be that little boy again.

What elated joy would that be, to smile once more with innocence and sleep with peaceful mind that I am safe cradled in my mothers arms.

Oh little boy come out from that hiding place for I seek to love you and embrace you. Do not be afraid of the world and longer.

I will protect you and keep you safe from harm, but there is no little boy. My memory is losing its substance and I again disappear into nothingness void of any knowledge of who I am or who I was.

I am there among the prairies, among once again with these mystifying and magical creatures who shift shape at will. They all surround me and howl and I am beheld by these soulful eyes. How I wish I can transform into a blazing Phoenix and engorged them within my searing fire.

Together we shall rise above all possibilities. I shall make a burning trail straight into the depths of the sun. But no, I am just a mere man forever in search of this true self.

~ *Dancing Cobra* ~

As Night Passes

∕∂

As night passes into early hours
of morning I sit searching.
The thought which lies just beyond the reach
of feelings that accompany them
As at times, my feelings take me
into unknown depths
and leave me grasping at straws of understanding
which pulls me into the embrace
of deep contemplation
where I'm left to explore what goes beyond sight
and sound and beyond the grasp of the mind.
Leaving me to seek the union of the soul
and the spirit
so they may discover
the potential of feelings…
Which led me here!!!

~ Unknown ~

The Day Lyle Went to the Hole

~

During war he's at home.
He executes the moves of victory
move-counter move.
He's fiercely calm in the fury.
The least amount of effort, maximized gain.
Shed the least blood, save the most men.
Being sensitive to loss at heart is valor.
His ferocity won't subside during peace time.
Habitual strategies wasted on unwaged wars.
His heart aches for the comfort of peace,
but he can't shake his training.
This Warrior King aches for the throne of peace
in the court of compassion,
casually exchanging heart talk
among friends not foes.

~ Healing Wolf ~

James

❧

I'm like a bucket of
water in prison who
would like to be poured
back into the streams of
life.

So I ask God almighty to
forgive me for pouring a
bucket of water in the
sand.

~ Dusty Husband ~

At the Institution for Emotionally Disturbed Adolescents

❧

Plastic wood paneling gives off
its pine disinfected resin.

Gray glare through partially
opened fold in thick protective
curtain (green in color)
reveals quiet hour for six hyper
kids, sitting in a circle on large
multicolored pillows as they try to count to ten,
without speaking.

So
Dora, eyes closed tight
makes it to five
when she is punched in the chest by Michael,
sitting next to her – he smirks at her flashing
eyes.

Brian tugs Stephen's head by his ear
and whoops excitedly to avoid a punch
with a pencil.

Sara and Denise hold on to dolls with uncommon
intensity, rocking in invisible chairs.

The supervising staff member shakes her head
with disapproval; "Shhh, children, quiet time…"
gives another sharp look and returns
to her book

~ *Patrick Nolan* ~

For Richard Samuel II

⁊

I yelled and cursed at you in anger
on the telephone Tuesday night.
I cut you off because you screwed things up
in much the way I screwed them up when I was 22.
It took me several days before I let that in;
that I too screwed things up at 22.

I've not lived well, but long enough to see the dark
and painful violence done to children in the name of love.
Your namesake, and my father, never lived that long;
he died of violations to his body and his soul,
his children and his wife.

Now I would break the chain of pain that runs
far back into the drunken past,
by giving voice to demons who insist on being heard;
perhaps not pleasant to the ear of silent generations.
But better said in verse and line
than on the phone
to one I love who died a little at the curse
of being told he'd made a small mistake.

~ Keeper of the Dragon ~

Caged Up

❧

Yeah its a cold fuckin' life caged up as a man,
not able to wonder free and be who I truly am.

At times I want to open that cage to my heart.
But to be honest, I am afraid men may tear it apart.

Then there's days I want to express my mind,
but by opening that cage it's against the rules of
doing time…

Sometimes I wonder why this must be.
But then I realize I did this caged up shit to me.

So here I am caged up as a man.
Wondering when I can be who I truly am.

Only time will tell,
if this caged journey leads to heaven or hell.

I know I want to be free,
and enjoy all of life's beautiful mysteries.

Who knows,
maybe these words are a start,
to tearing those cages apart?

So wish me well,
on this journey to heaven or hell.

And remember me,
as I struggle and fight to get free…

~ *Unknown* ~

Untitled Number Three

❧

Once I held a man's sorrow in my lap.
He trusted me not to break it
but to gently treat it with intense compassion.
With his pain I cried. With his sorrow I ached.
With my helplessness I loved.
My heart burst with joy,
to be his solace and sanctuary,
in the heart of our madness.
I live in the junk yard of people.
You know, the throw aways,
one's that're disposable –
my people.
I feel my heart's bursting joy,
is every bit as good
as the Squareheads on the streets.
Maybe better?

~ Healing Wolf ~

One Week Later

❧

I must dump the chaos,
to make room for peace.
Chaos clutters and clogs all of me,
and that asshole fear keeps interfering
with my growth.
I move
fear counter moves,
blocking my way.
Enough.
This must stop and it will,
damn it.
Priceless the glimpse of relief,
I've stumbled on.
When I pushed past that asshole fear,
sweet the taste of joy,
after bitter bouts with truth.
Fear tried to scare me,
with truth's ugly faces of pain,
the asshole.
Thank Spirit that I didn't back down,
...this time.

~ Healing Wolf ~

Where Will You Be?

❧

Deep deep down in the deepest depth,
in the hidden parts of my mind
I'm afraid.
I'm afraid I am gonna end up
standing in the center of the Circle all
abandoned by those I depend on.
My fear is
it's gonna turn out to be a lot harder than they planned on,
so they are gonna brake and run to something easier
instead of facing the fears of doing this work.
I get it, this work is hard.
In the deepest depths of my mind I am scared,
will I be the only one left?
And if I am what does that say about my hopes and dreams?
So in the deepest depths of my mind,
I am afraid…I am real afraid.
I don't think I can do this alone.
It's just not a one man job.
If I don't do it who will?
And will it ever get done?
I'm sure a lot of guys think so,
they think it will get done regardless of who does it,
and who knows they may even be right.
But in the deepest depths of my mind
I sure don't think so…
So I will keep stepping up
even when I ain't got a clue what the fuck I should be doing.
The only question I have is,
where will you be???

~ *Painted King* ~

Is It Weak

❧

Is it weak if I throw my head back and cry?
Is it weak if I slam my fist
Into the stone wall holding me in this prison cell?
Is it weak if I allow myself to feel how angry and sad I am?
Is it weak to know that when I thought I was so hard
I was just too weak to be who I should have been?
Tell me brothers is it weak for a convicted killer
To want to learn how not to be so cold and hard?
And is it weak that I don't care if anyone
And everyone thinks it is weak?

~ Painted King ~

I Statements

᷁

I'm not comfortable having to own and carry the weight of my own
words.

I'm not comfortable when others speak for me.

Conversations are more fun if I can slip and slide around shit,

Pulling the listener into my drag.

But being called on my drag with the 'I'

I'm usually tempted to avoid responsibility,

And temptation clouds my mind.

But the 'I' isn't part time, is it?

~ Healing Wolf ~

Away

~~

There once was this boy
who was as happy as a child could be.
The angels of heaven
turned their backs
to the perverted sexual acts
this man child performed on him.
You see this boy
knew these things were wrong.
He started acting out,
trying to get some genuine love;
he grew up
with too many ghosts in his closet.
He had no other way of expressing himself
so he started drinking, doing drugs,
feeding the demons he had in his soul.
The child still lives in the man
hidden from the world he acted out one too many times,
caused his loved ones to cry
locked away
like he locked away the pain, shame.
You see I can relate to this little boy;
the boy still lives in me.

~ Loving Leopard ~

Mask

❧

How should I feel
You jumping back
Into my life
Like a crazy ass jack in the box
Should I laugh and smile with joy
How can I forget all of my anger
I hide so easily from you
You ran off with my soul
Handing me back left over's of your love
I'm still pissed off at you
It's so odd
Your uncaring attitude
How can I pretend
That you never broke my heart
Please take off your mask
Show me
Who you really are.

~ Loving Leopard ~

Untitled Number Eleven

✎

Ugly hateful memories
I have of me
You have hidden yourself well
Mister who the fuck do you think you are?
A gangster
A Crankster
A heroin dope fiend
A thief
A womanizer
A fucked up father of four
A prisoner of the drug war
I fought on the streets
A war I continue to fight even in here
Who the fuck are you mister?
A sad little boy
Crying out in the dead of the night
For a father who's passed out
Crying out for your sister
Who's crying out for you
Your cry's interlocked for all eternity
Ugly hateful memories
I've hidden from you.

~ Loving Leopard ~

Unknown

❧

We are born like this
Into this, into these carefully made wars
Into the sight of broken dreams of emptiness
Into bars where people no longer feel comfortable speaking to one
another
Into fist fights that end in shooting and stabbings.
Born into this, into hospitals so expensive it's cheaper to die
Into lawyers who charge so much, I had no choice but to plead guilty.
Into a state where the jails are full, the madhouses closed!
Born into this walking and living through this
Dying cause of this, muted cause of this
Castrated, pummeled, jailed, accused, denied
Because of this, fooled by this, used by this, pissed on by this
Made crazy and sick by this
Made violent practically inhuman by this.
The heart is blackened, the fingers reach for the throat
The gun, the knife, the gun.
The fingers reach for the unresponsive God.
We are born into this sorrowful deadliness
We are born into a government 60 years in debt
That soon will be unable to pay the interest on that debt.

Banks will be robbed, money will be useless
Murderers will go unpunished
Due to guns and roving mobs
Food will become a diminishing return
The sun will not be seen and it will always be night
Trees will die, vegetation too.
Radiated men will eat one another
The sea will be poisoned
Lakes and rivers will vanish making rain the new gold; the rotting bodies
Of men and animals will stink in the wind
The last survivors will soon fall to unknown new disease.
When all is gone there will be the most beautiful silence ever heard.
Born out of that the sun still hidden nowhere
Awaiting the next chapter.

~ Silver Wolf that Cares for the Pack ~

Eyes Wide Open

~

My eyes are wide open.
I'm looking for love.
I'm seeking the one who cares that I feel alone.
I'm hunting the woman that wants to save me from myself
and my overwhelming sadness.
My eyes are wide open
and all they see is gray stone and razor wire,
steel locks and eyes with an empty lost look in them. My eyes are wide
open
and I clearly see the other wide open eyes
looking for love and seeking someone,
anyone to save us from all this sadness.
Everyone's eyes are wide open...
Is anyone's heart open???

~ *Painted King* ~

Looking Inward

≈

When you look inward what do you find?

Who looks back at you ?

Who is that person?

When you look inward, deep into your soul
What do you find?
Do you find someone you love?
Or do you find someone
Unknown to you?

When you look inward
What do you find?
Do you find someone with compassion,
Strength and integrity?

When you look inward
Do you see some one in love with life?
Someone who dares to
Dream?

When you look inward
Do you see someone who is
One with you
When you look inward?

~ Painted King ~

Dark Starless Night

꙳

Peering longingly into
Dark starless nights
Searching and seeking for answers
To all the questions in my head.
Peering into dark starless nights
Getting lost in the deep depths
Of creation.
Seeing past the darkness and seeing
The unknown, the movements that go unseen,
The worlds that no one understands
And yet they are.
Peering into dark starless nights
Searching for answers that
I don't need at all.
Seeking a more in-depth understanding
When in fact I don't even understand
My own mind
And just what it is that it can do.
Peering into the dark starless nights
And just now starting to see it

or what it is
Just a dark starless night...

~ Painted King ~

October – Month Ten

PRISON LIFE

Stone walls and concrete ceilings and floors, steel beds, lockers, and doors, with a view of fence and razor wire. Chains, shackles, cuffs, keys clanging, locked in a cage.

Prison is a school of hate. Those caged move to outdated rhythms and the places in the streets they come from. Rules are carved into bullet riddled walls. One convict's word can ruin the world of another. Attitudes are germinated in blood and fertilized in hate.

Everything is restrained, feelings, desires, urges, impulses, emotions; replaced with the many horrors, fears, anger-rage, depression, loneliness, and agony.

The meaning of time changes, consequences become bizarre and bizarre becomes normal. There are many ways minds deteriorate. Facades, masks, and images are adopted, there is no escape. Demons hunt, often bursting into bloody madness. There are many ways to die, on the inside, one moment at a time

What It Is

⌇

What it is, this ain't hell,
but even caves breed bats.
In the guts if cities things breed in thre dark,
rats and disease that feed in rivers of human waste
beneathe a concrete veil of clean-swept streets
and pretty pastel houses all in a row.
And this ain't hell.
This is just concrete.
This is just water under the bridge, a notch in the wrist,
a scar, a cum-soaked sock, a hiss in the night
when I'm afraid of death.
It's just a letter I didn't write, unsaid words,
like love, like later, like sorry, God.
Just a splinter in the eye, free to go mad,
free to chew my leg bloody
because I can
t drag the trap anymore.
It's just my teeth rotting, blood in my stool,
the apathetic, noose that hangs me every day;
the sins of my father, every nouveau guru telling me
"do this, read that, you're on the right road
but your walk's all wrong."
It's just Jung and the devil, and who failed who
while the Lamb of God points with wounded eyes
when I sing prayers in Celtic Blues
and eat his chalky bits of skin.
It's just a poet on the toilet getting fucked by the needle,
the wrong ride when you're hitchin',
a child in the trash; but this ain't hell.
This is just the way it is.

~ *Shaman's Key* ~

Welcome to My World

༂

Welcome to my world,
A resort of sorts you see.
Where at three the door will lock behind you and fantasies are free.

Where calendars mean nothing as months turn into years
Where memories can haunt you
And rivers flow from tears.

Where concrete walls surround you,
Cell bars of cold hard steel.
Your conscience starts to haunt you
And nightmares seem so real.

A domain filled with sorrow
Where men break down and cry,
A place with no tomorrow
Where people live and die.

Welcome to prison
A warehouse of human race,
Where even when someone's set free
Another takes their place.

So welcome to my world
If it's where you want to be
A barren cell,
A home in hell,
I pray they set you free.

~ Painted King ~

Chains of Bondage

~

Chains of bondage hold me tight,
for a war of pure delight.
With no escape and boundless rules,
I engage in a game meant for fools.
A demons rage builds deep inside,
full of passion I cannot hide.
A taste of flesh is what I desire,
but when I indulge it flames like fire.
Don't hold back the battle is on,
shed my blood before the moment's gone,
then taste your victory like it's the last,
because you'll be hit by my powerful blast.
In a flash of light you'll hit the floor,
like you've been struck by the almighty Thor.
Your most powerful climax will burst into flames,
making you shudder as you yank at the chains.
Chains of bondage holds me tight,
for a war of pure delight.

~ Unknown ~

Things to Mind

Two tiers-fifty cells-madness dwells

Speed babies-pushing rabies

Welcome to hell-lost soul-lose control

Can't blame fate-we create-contemplate

Your mind-your time-turn it around

Strong minds we waste-doing time always

This you'll find, things to mind...

~ Unknown ~

I Am Not a Prison Poet

I am not a prison poet.
I can't enchant you
with metaphors for grey
the image of a torn throat
or with a few words
cast the shadow of bars
across your face.
I can't stand
on a concrete soapbox
and tell you what's wrong
with society and God
or make the heart indignant
with tales of beaten dogs
because, like I told you
I'm not a prison poet;
and when I stand
in the shallow pit
we call a yard
I don't see a thousand stories
circling the track
but a great sadness
for the unretrieved
and I, a part of that sadness,
you, a part of that sadness
and I want
to lay it all down
but like I told you
I am not a prison poet.

~ Shaman's Key ~

When Night Time Comes

~

When night time comes here to our house, sometimes only sometimes if you listen real close when you think everyone is asleep, and all is quiet you can hear the tears and memories fall like rain. It happens late in the night, when men stare out cracks in concrete walls, and moonbeams fall across open mouths. It is a time when dreams pour like blood from the eyes of lost men, and the sounds of the past echo through trembling lips. Like old books put on the shelf, forgotten, untouched and covered with the dirt of time. Worn dusty faces, streaked with the sweat of unfinished promises, search the cold walls of their cell for something that is almost never found. A loving face from the past. A kind word from someone who used to care. A blessing from an unspoken prayer. The melody to a song that was never sung. The touch of a hand. The question. The answer. Hope. Peace. Never found. As night goes on, dirty feet are blistered from dragging across stone floors, and yellow teeth are worn down under grinding jaws. Broken knuckles are bruised and swollen under clenched fists from battling unseen devils that hide in the corner of your mind. All this goes on under the cold cover of darkness, when the moon is full and lost souls search the night for acceptance -Suddenly!!-
Down on the other end of the cell block, someone screams and shatters the silence like a mirror that has crashed to the ground and broken into a thousand pieces. It was a man being stabbed to death by his cellmate, he screams no longer, forever silenced. In another cell a man who is alone, swings from his neck kicking like an ugly rag doll. In his own way he has finally went home. In another cell a man just holds his head in his hands and weep, letting his loneliness flood through his veins like rivers of ice until his heart is finally broken. And in another cell a man in a twisted way laughs like a mad man, almost foaming at the mouth like a rabid dog. But is he laughing? Or is he really crying? -SSSSSSSHHHHHH-
Listen closely to the sounds of tragedy.

~ *Indio* ~

Untitled

୭

At times my mind plays tricks on me with candy col-
ored chalk lines, sprinkling forbidden pine needles that
cover my steps from my hidden secrets. The end of
my world starts to blend flashes of ice sickles, captured
in micro thought's that drive me to a single sentence
of apocalyptic climax. Slowly but surely my hand
begins to play out rhythmic jolts as the ink embeds
its commas and semi-colons in a down ward motion
of poetic vision. My mind drops in to the depths of a
realmless dream but my nimble fingers play a cordless
symphony mang the pages of my truth. It is at this
time that heart becomes an open door letting out the
pureness that dwells in my flesh. I begin to call out to
the four corners of a past life, as I sit back counting
the flecks of sand left in the hour glass. Penitentiary
pleasure swirls in the shadows as a ghetto child ignores
his potential, as the rose petals wither between the
iron mesh.

~ Puma Who Matters ~

Prisonface

~

He was born to this
he said often,
born to these rules,
these codes,
to the Prisonface,
the imprinted look of certain lines,
a certain geographical depth of eye sockets
a certain blankness of the eyes,
like broken windows in a new house.

He was born to this
by a mother's suicide,
a brutal stepfather's drunken fist,
to a world of howling Lostboys
scavenging in nightclubs, in pockets, in veins,
embracing shadow and fallen-ness
and quick to break the fingers
of those who brought him here.

~ Shaman's Key ~

V

❧

Squat monoliths stare unmoving beneath the rolling grey,
B-ball courts dark from last night's rain.
Steel mouths gape and spew humanity into a shallow basin
to endlessly walk a warped asphalt track
around and around and around
like Ixion to the wheel
like clockwork gears
like a snake devouring itself.
On dark courts dark men spit and bark
into their brother's face
while white men crowd a short wood bench
to flay a friend, to skin him alive,
as brown skins and red skins
and yellow skins slap blue balls against the monolithic face
that stares at them all close-mouthed.
And one might have been born
to old pale prisons with hand hewn walls of grey granite
and the striped shadow of cold iron doors;
old pale prisons full of echoes full of ghosts
full of faces hidden among forests of straight black bars;
to the jangle of keys to the night cries
to the fittest survives
and there's never a question of where you're at
until one day it's squat monoliths
and a big warped wheel and someone stands
among the orbiting flesh and says:
"where are you going?"

~ Shaman's Key ~

I Am a Storm

~

"I am a storm."
I am a storm that has passed,
and in the calm, the wreckage lays...
Hugo, Katrina, and Rita,
all rolled into one
testament to sheer audacity,
or in other words...
lack of forsight.

Things done that cannot be changed
indelible ink that outlasts
the desire and lifetime
of the one who applied it.

I am a storm
that is spent
and now resolve to see
the fledgling seeds
of a new hope
come to fruition out of passion came pain
and out of pain faith bloomed...
and its roots run deep...

~ Unknown ~

4:40 A.M.

∽

Nooks and crannies of this prison cell filled
with the energy of so many men
so many years.
I touch the gouge in the wall and almost see the
tortured soul teetering on the edge of insanity
as he pounds and pounds and pounds
the 8 ounce chili can,
trying to pound away the
wall standing between him and
the fact that
he will die in a box
just like this one.
Life means death to a convict.
4:40 A.M. Shadows carpet the cement floor
with the carefully laid Celtic knotwork paper tiles.
I feel the intense concentration of the man who spent
14 hours on his knees putting them there.
His own form of prayer.
Praying for compassion, praying that the demons
of his past will leave him alone and that his
god will give him some kind of peace.

He prays for the return of innocence.
4:40 A. M. I fill the warmth of redemption like a liquid
golden light washing over me warm and forgiving.
There are no words for the feeling of childish mistakes washing away.
No words for the bliss of hope, of love, of surrender of shame.
4:40 A.M. Moving past what once was,
it holds no energy it has no effect on what is.
Moving past plans of what will be,
the future has no depth, no weight; I can't touch it or control it
so I move past the imagined need to.
4:40 A.M. Right now is real and I chose to fill the nooks and crannies
of this prison cell
with the energy of love and peace of the calming feeling of right now.

~ Painted King ~

Light & Dark

*

Through chipped gray paint
sun rays struggle to shine.
Darkness retreats
at a less than
rapid rate.
In a prison cell
yielding comes hard
even to darkness.
Darkness clings tightly
to every surface to every corner.
Shadows dart and dance
all around the
piercing light beam.
Taunting the darkness
with it's abundance.
And still the light shines.
Growing and growing
brighter and brighter
pushing the darkness
further in to hidden depths.
As the shadows slowly
die to lights persistence
hope springs forth.
Warmth slowly creeps from
un-known hiding places.
Some times the darkness
does not
lose.

~ Painted King ~

Refraining Our Feelings

～

Our world has demanded that we refrain from showing who we are.
It's been this way so long that now when truth is shown in it's rawest
form the common reaction is fear. That forces us to retreat in to a safer
place where nothing touches our hearts.
So then there we sit in our safe self imposed hell pretending
we are doing just fine. Hiding, hiding from what's real. Hiding from
everything we feel.
And what if I jumped up and screamed? Or threw a chair or maybe just
told the world to shut the fuck up and take a look at what the hell we
have become.
Would I then be insane? Gone over the edge?
And if so over the edge of what?
And just what is the proper punishment for these souls who refuse to be
suppressed
and boldly allow themselves to feel the fuckedupness
of refraining our feelings?

~ *Painted King* ~

How Long

Put a man inside a cell how long before he begins to yell? Put a man inside a cage, and soon he will become overcome with rage. When the days turn to night how long before that man starts to fight?

When all is lost with nothing left to gain will that man show his pain? When he reaches out only to find there is no one there will that man no longer care?

I have seen men destroyed by dope but so much worse is a man who has no hope. When the walls start closing in then the madness begins.

You can be strong and overcome it all, but only if someone answers when you call. Who can say what loneliness cost? Who can say without it what will be lost?

I have lived in these cages for years, yet I still can't seem to overcome my fears. I have learned to live in my world of steel and stone, so why can't I learn to be alone?

So put me in a cage and force me to face my rage.
Put me in a cell to face my personal hell.

~ Painted King ~

Working Through Grief

❧

Cause the bunk.
The con clunking down
Steel stairs on his way
To sweep the tier;
Bland doughy
Faces of new commentators
Who set the stage
For the Unabomber trial;
I reach for a cigarette
Wrinkled denim
Lining of my jacket that hangs
From two dominoes glued
To the cell's unpainted wall
And light it up uncaring of the cigarette's stale acridness
Longing only for some gesture
Of reverence to her memory
I can offer upward, but all
I come up with is this poor poem.
Her last letter
Partially hidden
Under half written
Letters I leave
Buried unwilling
To feel anything
Other than the numb
Discerning fact
That she is no more;
Each stray thought
Speaks of her death
So I try to focus
On objects outside
Myself – the dope fiend
Whining for another fix.

~ *Patrick Nolan* ~

My Home They Built Around Me

A barren cell a hole in hell and I sit all alone,
For one small crime I pay with time where lights glare night and day,
And though I rage and pace my cage, I still must stay and pay.
My body cramps with cold that's damp and it chills me to the bone.
I hear the fling, the metal ring of keys and metal locks,
The scrap of feet upon concrete as guards patrol the blocks.
Convict's knifes take human lives no jungle holds more danger
And everyday that comes my way each man remains a stranger.
I watch my back 'cause there's a lack of men who can be trusted;
You know I kill and if I do I will before it's me that's dusted.
They came today to take away the man who lived next door,
To end his strife he took his life. He couldn't take no more.
I don't know who to tell this to 'cause most are only verses
That don't say much of anything and most are only curses.
So if something fatal should come my way should someone take life,
Just tell my mom I loved her so and also tell my wife
That I was glad for what we had and all they've done for me.
And though I'm gone one thing lives on, "My love eternally"
My one desire should I expire is that no one cry for me.
Just hold my mom within your arms and tell her that I'm finally free.

~ *King Panther Who Pours Love* ~

Ole Dog

~

Listen closely ole dog, to the sorrowful sound, the catcher has come to
mark his grounds.

Stale food throwed upon a tray, scraps of meat and bone along with
tooth decay.

Dusty mutt, mangy ole hound, locked in a cage like lost and found.

Keys clanging tied to his hip, always stays out of reach so he can't get bit.

Your howl comes from a wicked place, love and laughter not a trace.

Bark and growl, snarl and bite, the life you live is a constant fight.

I understand my four legged friend, the pain in your heart, and the
pound you're in.

I live in a place like yours, locked in a cage with iron doors.

~ Indio ~

Sweet Sorrow

❧

Sweet, sweet sorrows, how I love your bitter taste on my blistered lips. Bathe my soul in misery let the tears of loneliness quench my thirst until I drown.

Fall down upon my skull with all that is hated, let the wicked fingers of pain massage my rotten flesh. Cover me in a blanket of regrets, with tiny lights of shame.

Break my teeth with the bones of the dead, let their haunting screams forever dance upon my chest.

Let the faces and the songs of the past pierce my blackened heart and cause it to beat no longer.

Lay my diseased body down in a cold bed of stone. Let no one walk by and no love ever show.

Let the beasts of the forest devour what is left. Make my soul wander forever searching, never to find rest.

Let the stench of my memory echo in the brains of the men and women who imprisoned me and drove me insane. Let the sound of agony become my name, listen closely.

Let my name ride upon the wings of evil and become a plague upon the earth, inflicting open sores on all those hold the keys.

Walk with me my imprisoned brothers, let us bask in the sweet sorrow that is ours and let us all drink from the fountain of hunger and embrace that which kills us.

Somebody asked me if I felt like I have paid for my crimes?
"Paid in full I say!"
Just look what I've done to myself.

~ Indio ~

Do You Know?

❧

Do you know?
Because if you truly knew, then please believe that there wouldn't be any
doubts or questions, on these various words that reflect and express who
I am.
A true bond is unbreakable, and I know my life sometimes is, and may
always be unexplainable.
Yeah, I have sat down, talked, and really got to know and understand
change.
Or should I say he has got to know me. And all my struggles and pains-
because those eyes in the mirror still look the same.
Do you know?
What has meaning to me? What matters? And what dumb shit that I'll
never let stress me out.
"Think" why would I sacrifice the only real thing of value that I have
left?
Not knowing if in fact it's me that matters most.
I bleed my heart into every word hoping that you'll look deeper and my
chance start to understand my soul.
Yeah. I do fear never really being understood, remembered as just
another real "nigga" who lived and died in the hood.
Do you know
that I sometimes lay and cry in the dark saying prayers, wondering if
"Allah" is listening to my thoughts, knowing I've seen and been through
a lot.
Lost amongst men with no voice and little hope of ever seeing freedom
again. Men who've sinned, and because of the concrete many refuse to
look in. Even at their own kin. I guess because they fail to realize that
this is the end, going to sleep and praying never to see daylight again.
Do you know
that this is who I am and how sometimes I feel?
Do you know?

~ *Young Life* ~

True Depth

❧

Seeking the true depth of my compassion
hunting for years looking for the inner love
that at times overwhelms me
like the sight of a child being born into this world.
Sitting in circles placing myself in places
where the nameless god walks and talks
where on the right days and at the right times
when men move beyond fear and ego
I can feel the fingertips of spirit's love brush my heart ever so lightly.
Wiping away years of doubt and frustration
that prison has pounded and pounded into my head.
I cling to a sacred part of myself
That is the true depth of who I am.
Of who you are of who we all are.

~ *Painted King* ~

Ol Mister Crazy

In a mist of madness a fog so thick
You can't see the face of ol mister crazy.
You hear his steps as he walks the tier
Always getting closer
But never quite getting to your cell.
It's said that ol mister crazy
Has already touched all of us when we first got here.
Remember that cold spot you walked through on your way in?
That was a slight caress from his hand of madness…
Ol mister crazy he's a sly one,
He don't hurry.
Sometimes he takes years to do his dirty work.
Just a little bit at a time
Ol mister crazy knows how to make you lose your mind.
And before too long
Ol mister crazy
Will be the only one who can understand you…

~ Painted King ~

Other Side of the Glass

The other side of the glass
there's so much to distract us
even under the worst of conditions
the way any prisoner does
able to recall the scent of old lovers
long gone, long dead.
Viewed with a certain kindness we drift
willing to take refuge anywhere
backward, forward, anywhere but here.
Backward into the handful of few places
where kindness and laughter and love
momentarily bumped into us
from around a blind corner.
We conveniently leave out
the part where they invited us to join them
but we declined as we politely dusted off any secret desires
to go racing after them as they disappeared into the crowd.
Or forward maybe
we drift into the tattered remains of what we'll do
if we can ever get out of this cell.

It's too painful it seems
to awaken again and again and face this bone numbing isolation.
So we co-create whole worlds made to drift in.
Expect I can't do it anymore and neither can some of you.
Not anymore.
I can't do what most people call life.
It's like looking through glass meant to be painted
and so from time to time when I have the courage
or have lost the strength to do otherwise
I step through and lie down naked and defeated
and feel what I feel.
All if it.
It's terrifying and wonderful, even if just for a moment,
to finally rest cradled in the other world.

~ *Lion Who Sometime Catches Fire* ~

Happy Birthday

∼

Today is my forty-second birthday. And once more I find myself spending it within the confines of a prison cell. It seems that I should be some what unhappy about that, but in truth I am not. I am sitting right this second just where I need to be sitting to fully feel who I am.

I am a good person.

I did not always believe this to be true. Yet today, today on the birthday I find myself looking back over my life from I see and more importantly feel that indeed it's true.

I am a good person.

I have lived a life full of adventure and thrill, both good and bad. I have seen killers with a golden glow worthy of a saint. I have felt tears of joy stream down my cheeks more than once. I have thrown back my head and laughed with the glee of a child.
I have seen gods eyes in mere men. I have felt gods hands holding my heart. I have been blessed many times by great men. My life is indeed a gift.

I am a good person.

I watched a dragon come alive many times. I watched the things that can't be done get done every week. I took part in the birth of and protection of something that is bigger then I will ever be. I have almost forgotten who I once was. I see who I can someday become.
And right now.

I am a good person.
Happy birthday to me.

∼ Painted King ∼

Clinging

~

Clinging to the forgotten and rotten beliefs that I have to be someone
important or I am no one.
For who will love me if they know I am not
a cold heartless killer any longer?
Will you still show me the same amount of respect when you know
there is no longer a threat of me ripping your throat out?
Clinging to forgotten and rotten beliefs
that I have to be someone strong, someone who knows
how to put my fist firmly through your face.
Letting go of rotten but not forgotten beliefs that I must be feared to be
liked.
I refuse to cling to that
lie any longer…
I am not clinging. Not now. Not ever again.
I clung for way to long; I now know the clinging was wrong.
I wont cling, I am way too strong.

~ Painted King ~

Walking in Circles

❧

I have walked for miles and miles
in circles
for years and years
I have walked in circles.
I walked many prison tracks
from one end of the state
to the other.
Always walking in circles.
I walked circles in the snow
I walked circles in the
desert heat.
But I was always
walking in circles.
And from one end
of the state to the other
all the circles felt
just the same.
Round and round
and all the circles led to the same
fucking dead ends.
Regardless of how many miles
or how many hours I walked
I never got any further away from
where I started.
So now I find my self sitting in circles.
I got some miles on this old chair I am sitting in.
I think after all these years of
walking in circles
if I sit here and
look inside
I may finally cover some ground.

~ Painted King ~

Golden Light

෨

Some place in a cold gray stone world
On a cold rainy winter day.
A man sits engulfed in a golden light.
A slight smile crosses his face
As he thinks of all the magic he has
Seen in this drab place.
For this is prison;
How can a man be at all content?
This is madness.
Or is this perhaps
hope at work?
Who in there right mind
Can throw back their head and laugh at life?
Who in their right mind dares to find
Goodness in the world's throw away?
I see the light that saves souls.
I see the compassion in killers.
I see maybe for the first time
In my life I see.
I know the power of the golden light.
I have felt it's goodness wash over me
Cleansing me to the very core
Of who I am.
And I smile a slight smile
Because it is just so
Damn funny to me
That I had to come to prison to see
This kind of goodness...

~ *Painted King* ~

Looking Beneath the Surface

❧

Under the scars and tattoos
Dwells a man who cares.
Under the hate and the anger
Lives love and compassion.
Under the mask of 'fuck-it, I just don't care.'
Lives hope and dreams.
Under the I don't need anyone' role I play
Is a desire to trust.
Under the blood stains on my hands
I find shame.
Under the cold outside
Is a man who needs to be loved.
Under the biker, killer, convict,
Is a father, a son, a brother, an uncle and a friend.
I'm like a bucket of water in prison
Who would like to be poured back into the streams of life.
So I ask God Almighty to forgive me
For pouring my bucket of water in the sand.

~ Painted King ~

Lower Our Masks

⌖

Let us as men lower our masks.
Let us show our truths,
Let us as men
Step away from the heartless animals we must be,
In this den of madness.
If only for a little while,
Let us as men of strength show our souls.
Let us as men of power extend our hand
Without it being firmly wrapped around a scrap of prison steel.
Let us as men of wisdom and compassion
Take a youngster and teach him of life
Instead of cutting bloody furrows into his body
As we take his life.
Let us as men of honor forget the hustle,
Let us go beyond race
Or who we worship or what the homeboys think we should do
Or the prison bullshit.
Let's as men for once look at our needs
To become the men we know we could have been
And should have been.
Let us as men of chance bet on ourselves,
Let us trust each other,
Let us spin the wheels
For once give something of ourselves away.
Let us men lower our masks…

~ *Painted King* ~

Sitting Still

❧

Sometimes I got to sit still, sometimes I got to be alone just sit still
and feel what my spirit has to say to me.
When the prison crap starts drenching my soul
and the demons of hate, anger, racism and fear tries to rip my eyes out
so I can no longer see the goodness around me anymore.
I got to sit still, I got to be alone and feel what my spirit has to tell me.
It's true I love my brothers each and every one. I want to feel what they
feel and I want to hear their words. I want to know their hearts as I
know mine.
Yet at times my own brokenness stands in my way. When the racial
warrior or the prison bullshit enters I just got to sit still.
Sometimes I got to be alone and just feel what my spirit has to say to me.
At these times my spirit tells me "Love be real and never give up."

~ Painted King ~

Passing It On

❧

I remember
it happened to me
I was eighteen
couldn't be told
anything about anything

out of fear
or because I was afraid
I wound up
inheriting the ways
of thought, of survival
of protection and spending
years alone with my own
isolated ideas

when in my cell
I got a youngster
I was reminded of the legacy
how we breed
when we are hardened.
and what it will be

that I pass on.

~ Silver Wolf that Cares for the Pack ~

Hope

It's not about the amount of pain I have felt.

It's not about the amount of shame I have felt.

It's not even about the amount of sorrow I have felt.

It's about hope.

It's about strength.

The strength to plow through the pain, shame,

and sorrow of a life time and still be able to hope.

It's hope in a place like this that

keeps men from being eaten by their shadows.

~ Painted King ~

November - Month Eleven

PRISON LIFE

The cold cover of night-time hides the unending restlessness, waking to the same nightmare every morning. A part of us died when we entered prison. Becoming strangers to our own families, and endless wondering in our old thoughts and wars bottled deep within. They think we are twisted because we think this shit is fun.

Now time is all we have and sometimes we escape our harsh reality through sleep. In prison hopes become spaces in the thick fogs of madness. Saints here carry clubs.

Drugs and the sweaters who the fiend avoids, if he can, while looking for his next fix. Bigots of convenience pimp out outfits. Everything is noticed by furtive eyes. The homeless hearts haunting these cages, no-one trusts, while fermenting into nothingness.

Refusing to let our will be crushed, we pretend to be strong, and cling to nostalgia. A life sentence means a living death to a convict.

We consider the many ways to ask for God's forgiveness and hope to feel his fingertips brush our heart while the crime is paid for.

Ironically, when we step out of the dark and out of our addiction to misery, we decide to care, and are surprised that nobody notices.

The pains that consumed me and the agony of my own life, let me forget what it is to be me.

Dark

❧

I have written sweet sounding poems where nightmares are transmuted into soothing dreams. I have written about hate and despair magically becoming tender love. I even wrote about butterflys and bunnies and every thing was good. Not all poems are good after two decades of bad. Tell me about love when every where you go your drenched in hate. When the only butterflys you know are the ones in your gut. The only rabbit you know is what you need to know how to do when shit goes sideways in front of you. Tell me how to write about angelic things when most of the time all I see is demented demons. How do I write about hope when all I see is destruction? Where is it OK for me to be dark? To be sad, mad, fed-up wore out and flat out pissed off? Who can sit in that shit without fixing me or looking at me like I have just became some kind of creature of doom?

Just for the record a part of me is dying a slow hard death, my saint got raped by false hope and bullshitting free people. I feel betrayed in the worst way. Love is a lie. A lot of people love me. A lot of people lie. Welcome to the badlands. Saints carry clubs here. Betrayal has a price. I may choose to love you. Understand that I will not trust you. Not any of you. Love cuts deep into the soul, and lies cut deep into a man who lives by his word. I know not one person who can be trusted with the power over my word, not one. Welcome to the badlands, I'm wore out. I'm dark right now. And that is just what I want to be today. That too is an aspect of my environment. The tower cop, the yard cop, every over paid piece of shit in my life is dark and rotten. So don't act all shocked when it effects me.

~ *Painted King* ~

Reflections

❧

You there
You despicable little fuck
You did the crime
Time is all you have now
You're scared again
Why now?
You acted tough on the streets
You cried for help
It fell on deaf ears
Thinking to yourself
Your family, wife, kids,
Are better off without you
You think that bullshit
Deep down you know the truth
I've stepped away from the mirror
I don't like who I see.

~ Loving Leopard ~

The Struggles of Our Mind Against Insanity

❧

To act insane, abnormal
What a joy
To cross over
And not look back.
To be released of the patterns
Of everyday worries.
Behave like a clown,
Like a wild beast
Without regard for all those eyes…
Walk around with no hurry,
But with ease…
Know of no dead.
And re-center the soul within.
Behave!
But die alive.

~ Fierce Fox ~

Pretend

❧

You pretend, CDC pretends, my Mom and Dad pretends,
my Sister pretends, my Wife pretends, my Son pretends,
but worst of all is I pretend.
Well damn it, it's not okay.
It's not okay that I'm alone,
It's not okay that I'm locked up in this fucking box,
when I could be helping my Mom and Dad and my Wife and Son.
It's not okay that I am a stranger to my own family.
I pretend I'm rock solid strong and brave
when the truth is I am scared shitless
that I'm gonna grow old and die,
in this hate filled house of fakeness,
to have it end with a phone call by some suit and tie
who didn't even know who the fuck I was.
I pretend I am calling the shots in my life
when the truth is, it's all out of my hands.
Everything I have done this far can be taken away from me
by one no caring son of a bitch
who has given up on himself and on life.
How much control would I have

~ Painted King ~

Danger's Gate

Every day danger is found close at hand.
And every day danger makes his violent demand.
It don't matter what I think or how I may feel.
Cold heartless danger controls my will.
You may think we as men are the masters of our own fate.
I too once thought that way
but that was before I passed through danger's gate.
Once here they strip you of all your pride.
When you passed through danger's gate a part of you died.
All this steel and all these locks
now my body rots in this cement box.
As my skin begins to fade and turn pale
I fully realize that I am in hell.
Cop's everywhere every time I see them I hate them a little more.
That too is a gift from danger.
The sad part is he has so much more in store.
When I go to the yard with danger he will try to get me shot.
And even if I avoid the guns it's all on film so I know I am caught.
After the fight I look at the gunner and laugh
"Sorry fucker, you missed"
With pride in my heart me and danger walk away
with cuffs biting into my wrists.
Yes once more I danced with danger and almost got away.
But I won't smile too big
we do this crazy ass shit over and over every day.
Welcome to danger's gate,
now I know my fate.

~ *Painted King* ~

They Think

What I felt and what I have known are things I have never shown. To show these things even in part is to let someone into your heart.

They think you do what you do to be cool, they think since you have honor and pride you're a fool.

They can't understand how things ever got this far. They don't understand this is prison; things are not always up to par.

They think I forgot what I want in life. How in the hell could I ever forget my son or my wife? They are the providers of my hopes and dreams. It's them that give me the strength to endure the never ending screams.

They can't see that I am doing what must be done, they think I am so twisted I think this shit is fun.

They think because of me they are lonely if they lived a day of my life they would see I think of them only.

It's a hell of a joke and a cold twist, but in order to get home to them I must use my fist.

They think when it comes to fighting I crave it so my true feelings instead of sharing them I may as well just
save it.

~ *Painted King* ~

Seeking the Life I Was Born to Live

~

I seek the life I was born to live. I want the love that I should of had all of my life. Where do I go to find this kind of peace and compassion? Will any one ever give me that much understanding? Will any one ever truly want to know what I am feeling or what I am doing with my life?

I find myself looking at the men in this cold cement world that I find myself dwelling in. I wonder who loves them? who cares what they feel or think? Will any one ever show them that much understanding?

I sometimes cry tears for the man who is so hurt and been betrayed so many times that they will no longer allow men like me or any one to care for them or about them in fear of being further betrayed.

I seek the life I was born to live. I am afraid that the life I was born to live will turn out to be one that no one will let me care or try to understand the sadness they feel. If this is what my life is then what hope do any of us have? Have we became so cold and afraid that we will no longer let any one care or love us?

Oh god what have we done to our selves? Why must we push each other away? Why can't we stop hurting each other? Why can't I let you love me and why can't you let me love you?

It does not have to be this way at all. We could if only we would be such caring men. I know how to love. I have not forgotten no matter what the world has done to me and what I have done to myself and what I have done to so many others. That does not mean I can not be what I want the rest of the world to be.

I seek the life I was born to live. I seek the compassion that I know I am capable of giving. I seek the compassion that I know others are capable of giving. If we could just stop dwelling on the shit we have done in the past or stop dwelling on what we should do in the future and stand up like men and be the people we know we should be, then we all could find that compassion we seek.

But let me be real clear. You me and the rest of the fucked up cowards in this world are just way too busy putting our shit off on every one else to fully realize that we are the only ones stopping us from finding the compassion we tell our selves we seek.

No one will love us when we do not even like our selves...

~ Painted King ~

Untitled Number Three
❧

What any of it means,

nor the meaning of my life

spent almost totally

behind prison bars, which now

is faced with it's demise.

Yes. Soon I will be dead.

And yes I am scared.

~ Patrick Nolan ~

I Care

❧

I pretend I don't care, I pretend I don't care who hates who.
I pretend I don't care who's cold or hungry, I pretend I don't care
who's sad and alone or even those on the brink of their own destruction.
But it's all a lie because I do care. I care a lot.
I care that my parents are getting old and I am not there to help them.
I care that my wife is stressed out alone and afraid she will go crazy with
the sadness of knowing she will be alone for the rest of her life.
I care my little three year old son is now seventeen facing a mad world
fatherless
because I did not care when I should of.
I sit in my tiny cement box and think of all the things I do care about.
But CDC do not see it. Sometimes I want to scream
"WHY CAN'T YOU SEE I CARE! WHAT THE FUCK DO I
NEED TO DO SO
YOU AND EVERY ONE WILL FINALLY SEE THAT I DO CARE"
I care that I can not be apart of society,
I care that I have to live in a world of hate fighting insanity.
Damn it I care.

~ Painted King ~

Look at Me

❦

Look at me. Take a real good look at me.
Now be honest tell me what it is you think you see.
Don't be afraid, tell me what you think.
I know you only see a man covered in prison ink.

Did you notice my wedding ring?
Did you notice my sons face tattooed in to my side?
Did you notice the tombstones of my dead brothers
tattooed in to my flesh?
Look at me! Take a real good look at me
and tell me what you think you see.
Did you notice the tattoos that tell who I rode,
fought and was willing to die for?
Did you see the tattoo that tells how I fought the
courts who wanted to kill me in the name of justice?
Did you by chance notice the "die free" tattooed
on my hand to remind me of my dreams?
Did you see the tear tattooed under my eye
for all the tears I can never cry?
Look at me!
I'm so much more than
just a man covered in prison ink...

~ Painted King ~

Die

    ∿

I'm confused.
I can't hide any longer.
My thoughts
Find me everywhere I go.
Instead of pills making me believe
Everything's alright
They should have pills
To make you forget
Of love and your regrets.
I've destroyed
One too many lives.
I broke my children's hearts.
If I had to die
For them to have a better life
I'd put my head on the chopping block.
What good am I
Locked away.
It causes me pain
To think of them crying
Over the loss of me.

~ Loving Leopard ~

You

~

I think I've lost my mind
How can I lose something I've never had
I hunger for my own thoughts, emotions
It hurts to think about you
Will you please give me back my soul
Every time my heart beats
I hear your name in my veins
Even as I sleep
You invade my dreams
I hope you and the girls are okay?
That's the least I can do for you
Every time the man in green walks by with a stack
I hold my breath, my heart stops
Hoping for a card, letter
A postcard with the words: Fuck off
You at least owe me that much
I don't need money, food
I just need a few words
From you

~ Loving Leopard ~

Thunder Night

❦

A loud noise woke me up from a dreamless sleep

I sat up wondering why

The rumbling, bunk shaking sound interrupted

My much needed escape from reality

You see day-in, and day-out my life

Is filled with constant screams. talking

About shit that makes me want to go deaf

TV's and radio's turned up to the distortion point

You see people in prison spend most of their time

Trying to drown out the sorrow and pain they feel

So I compare music and talking

To the loud wonderful sounds of the heavens

You see someone up there needs noise

To distract his own thoughts.

~ Loving Leopard ~

Untitled Number Nineteen

Missing everything that's real to me

Wishing for things that's impossible to achieve

Sentenced to death

Without dying

Rage builds up to the point of agony

Wanting to change

Lack of understanding keeps me the same

I hate more than I ever did before

I took out my frustration on another

Couldn't deal with myself

So I focused on you.

~ Loving Leopard ~

Prison

❧

Prison is a second by second assault on the soul
A day by day degradation of the self
An oppressive steel and brick umbrella
That transforms seconds into hours
And hours into days
While a person is locked up in here
In this distant, cold netherworld
Time stands still
Children left on the outside grow into adulthood
Often having children of their own
Once loving relationships wither into yesterday's dust
Relatives die
And their loss is mourned in silent loneliness
Times and temperature change
And those who are caged move to outdated rhythms
Encased in a psychic cocoon of negativity
The bad only get worse
And the twisted become warped even more
Empty unproductive hours
Turn into years of nothingness
The mind–numbing, soul–killing savage sameness
That makes everyday an echo of the previous day
Makes prison the home of spirit death.

~ Midnight ~

Beyond Stone Walls

Peering far beyond stone walls and wire fences
I find in my mind's eye
Great sights.
Here in this place exist things of
Of unimaginable beauty;
Birds with glittering and glowing feathers
Fish of all sizes with florescent scales
Of pink, yellow, red and blue
Big light fluffy clouds float like marshmallows
In a cup of cocoa on a winter's day.
In this place both deer and dog run and play as one.
Nipping and kicking in
Playful glee
The grass
Ever so green sways and dances
The leaves of the trees
Sing with the gentle breeze
Animals of all sizes and shapes
Run and romp testing
The limits of their
Agility
Awe, the joy of
Peering far beyond stone walls
And fences of wire.

~ Painted King ~

Untitled Number Four

＞

I sleep with the tip
of a wolf's tail tucked
under the head of my mattress,
and on the wall opposite my bunk,
A calendar photo of a gray wolf
looks down on me in a poise that
could bolt at the slightest provocation.
I don't dream as I once did,
and the pain that once consumed me is but
a dull bearable thud behind blood-shot eyes.

Time is the teller of all
truth, with the remains
of mine, hollow ring on impact.
Fraud—turn sideways and vanish.
I am nothing, a product of social
charity—a beggar too afraid to ask,
too ashamed—look at me, in bed
poking around the canvas for last
images to display—sickening forgery,
like an upraised pup.

~ *Patrick Nolan* ~

Untitled Number Five

❧

I love the dark
It's peaceful
Stuck in neutral
No worry's
No pain
Lost my way
Alone
See you in the end
Craziness
Suicidal
Lost my way, find out why I'm alive
Why this happened
No lies
Truth
You're addicted
To misery
Cry for yourself
Beautiful, ugly
Alive, dead
The Middle
Prison

~ Loving Leopard ~

Front

❧

Why do we fight amongst ourselves
I'm having problems doing my own time
You put your own neck on the line
I didn't get high
On the drugs you got on a front
You have all the excuses down to a science
Mom's in the hospital
Sister's too lazy
Money's on the way
You've sold your TV, your tunes
Now you're trying to get rid of your celly's
fucked up Tennis shoes
Now your people, their people are sweating you
Get the money or else
Now you're on the way to see the MTA
Tooth brushes were made for your mouth
Now you got one residing in your neck
The only thing on his mind
When he can get his next FIX

~ Loving Leopard ~

A Clown's Way

~

Keep love in your heart
For the rest of your broken down-clown life everyday
Keep the good words you speak today
And fuckin' every tomorrow
And don't show what you ain't really today
If you're a drug addict, so fuckin' be it
Till you blow your damn veins away
Or stupid liver away—to death
Or don't fuckin' even touch poison at all
You wanna be the clown who giggles
And spits good times around the fuckin' crowd-
So fuckin' be it.
Who cares what another convict says about your good times
Fuckin' good
Good behavior will not drive you to shit you don't wanna smell
Your friend, mamma, father, sisters, brother, granny,
Grandpa, aunties, cousins, hoodrats, girlfriends,
Wife is having a bad day
Let their stupid rage
Sadly moment swell
And blow the fuck up, 'cause I care less
You're a good fuckin' stupid clown
Who lives in good times
And are a convict
And has lived this stupid happy way
Every fuckin' year
So continue
Fuck your friend in stress
And in depressed universes
But you continue living a world of smiles
And in remarks that will fuckin' mark your stupid friend
And families' brains away

~ *Significant Elk Who Soars* ~

Prison Ain't No Country Club

❧

No matter what they say.
All he had going
for himself
was a homemade outfit
he pimped out on the tier
for a fix, and that he lost today.

He knows. He says
it often enough. Eighteen
years doing time, chasing
the bag and no light in sight
of ever getting out.

He'll die in this place.
His urn of ashes, buried
in a numbered marker grave.

Fuck it, he says.
I don't give a fuck
Fuck all these mother fuckers.

His pleasures are few;
NFL season, wine, candy.
Heroin rules him—all else
comes second–last.

He denounces the lames,
rats and punks–a bigot of convenience
when it comes to the connection.

~ Patrick Nolan ~

Smiling

❧

I remember the room.
Portable classroom.
Flag in the corner.
Pinched-face spinster
diagramming sentences.
You smiled at me;
I gave you my heart.

There were lots more rooms.
Apartments in the city,
houses in the town,
trailer by the river,
beat-up
Volvo wagon.
No matter where we were
your smile lit up the room.

Then came the final scene.
Piss-stained mattress.
Broken bottles.
Soot-stained cookers and
many orange caps.
The room was on fire
but you kept smiling.

~ Unknown ~

Help

❧

I'm angry at the world
I'm too fucked up
To live in society
Violent actions
Took me away from the family
I can't help but feeling sad
At my bleak world
I call home
No place for love left in my heart
Lost hopes keep me awake
Sleep has lost its love for me
My old life is but a dream
Summers are always hot in my box
I call my new life
Winters are as cold as my memories
Of what I used to be
Your last touch has faded
I try to keep my mind bare
My soul is starting to wonder
To the land of the dead
I envy a cold dead sleep.

~ Loving Leopard ~

Cry Along With Me

~

My visions are stark mad with delusions of peace.
These streets are ruled by guns and drugs, slugs that
tugs at flesh and rip through vests in these infested
slums. Come and witness what I see.

Everyday I pray but God apparently ignores my
plea. There's only misery ahead for me. I brace myself
and wait for impact; my back's broken from the weight
of the world, and hoping this burden I'm holding
will ease up from these shoulders. Nothing is more
colder when a body goes into shock, wide eyed and
bloodshot; frantic breathing! The block taped up with
caution. A Mother is pleading for her son's wounds
that's bleeding.

Throwing curses to God, doctors and nurses. Death
has no purpose, so let me try to give some meaning
in these verses, give it new birth before they murder
us. I shall further explain, my pain shall nevermore
endure in vain.

God is coming! And I anticipate to dissect his
brain. Why we were born to suffer because the color
of our skin? A Khmer man in a white land with so
much pressure to sin. So who wins and loses? The
path each man chooses. The devil's road is ruth-
less. The truth is, it's hard when the odds are stacked
against us. Plus stuck on welfare, I sold drugs to make
the game fair, while breathing polluted air. Nobody
cares! The fact remains; the change is slow too many
people are dying, but nobody knows. Pain runs deep
in these streets. The world sleeps and I weep, long
nights alone with only faith to keep me strong. Hope
for a brighter tomorrow.

How can that be, I question?

~ Dancing Cobra ~

The Dead Seem to Rise When Least Expected

Floundering, I can think of no better way to describe it. He looked like one of those Greenpeace images caught on film to evoke moral outrage at the brutal atrocities senselessly inflicted on one of God's own: a sea lion beached and ensnared in a fishing trawler's lost seaweed tangled net, barking out pitiably with its few remaining gulps of breath.

I can't explain it any better. And even now, after all these many years that have helped to harden my heart against the sudden violent images so quick to pierce the eye; even now laying awake in bed late into the cell block tier in an eddying puddle spewing forth from a knife wound slammed once twice through the heart.

God, I wish I could paint a picture with these words capable of capturing what I see each time I slip into this reverie: how his right ankle was broken and in a cast; he lay on his side legs scissoring uselessly for leverage as he tried to push himself up, but with each feeble attempt his hands would slip in the warm slick pool oozing out of him, causing him to flop helplessly chest down into the bloody mess, his mouth working silent pleas.

I could only stand there, seven cells away and look on bound by the laws of the environment more eunuch than man.

I don't know why he had to die but with his sanction I am forever haunted by those last few seconds before the eclipse settled over his hazel eyes which locked onto mine till I no longer existed in the gazed and far away vision now focused on dimensions only the dead perceive.

(For Henry Sianez)

~ *Patrick Nolan* ~

369

Another Brother Falls

Another brother falls to the obligation of anger.

The rules are carved into bullet riddled walls,

when in disagreement we must strike out with a fast fist

smashing and beating our side into the man

who dares to disagree with us.

Another brother falls to the obligation of anger,

it don't matter that the disagreement is stupid,

that means nothing to nobody,

yet the rules are there.

So in order to maintain our positions we strike out.

Bathing our sadness in blood and it don't matter who's blood,

just so I don't have to be sad...

~ Painted King ~

Thickheaded

☞

My Tyrant sees someone headed for a wreck,
automatically he believes he has the right
to interrupt, correct, school or advise.
That's someone that didn't ask for his help
but he just had to speak.
He thinks he knows what's best for everyone.
He doesn't really care for them,
he just wants to hear himself speak,
to say smart things out loud, to impress those someone's.
This Tyrant is my Shadow, in love with his own voice.
Looking for excuses to show off his disgusting self,
to someone, anyone, it doesn't really matter,
the dumb bastard thinks he's smart.
If the poor someone even fakes to pay attention,
this Shadow Tyrant will ramble on and on,
loving his obnoxious arrogance.
Keeping the floor to speak as long as he can,
this Tyrant refuses to see this as arrogant behavior
vehemently defending himself.
Using any excuse,
to listen and love himself.
Puffing up his ego,
the thickheaded ass…

~ Healing Wolf ~

Locked Away

∼

I've heard there's a party up in the sky
waiting there for us when we die.
They say that time is on our side
But here, it is something used to divide.
It separates us from one another
Sister from Brother, Children from Father.
They give us a number and take away our name
then they put us in cells that all look the same.
We are locked away for error or for sin
and they don't give us credit for what's within
they say we are weak because we did wrong
but they don't realize that we are strong.
We survived the elements, we know the streets.
Most of us know what it's like to have nothing to eat.
They put us in here and say we live grand
but it would be different if they gave us a hand.
There is so much to say, so much to be heard
but they won't listen, they won't hear a word.
Our life behind bars is so unreal
they don't understand, they don't know how we feel.
I know how it feels, I know what I say
because you see, I am here, I am locked away.

∼ Midnight ∼

A Rant

⁓

I was invited,
truth to be heard,
to be welcomed;
doubt nags about the invitation.
Solemn silences, long faces, make me wonder?
Pains of their own paths?
Healing of their own medicine?
Experience between knowing & understanding?
Are these danger signs?
Is the welcome mat being rolled up?
But the secrets aren't hidden anymore,
they're out in the open.
Are my shadows too powerful?
Is my suffering too intense?
Are you back peddling?
Screaming in fear that you'll withdrawal…
Maybe I shouldn't of answered the invitation?
Where's the strength, the power, the magic?

~ *Healing Wolf* ~

Yeah That's Bullshit

❧

Sometimes I can't stand the agony of my own life

seeing in the darkness what's too ugly for the light.

Giving up on myself, dancing.

Questioning the questions.

My shit is different, you can't fix it.

It won't get better, and I'd rather cheat myself,

then suffer the relief.

This bullshit is killing me.

I don't appreciate the pain,

but I need the relief.

The bullshit is, I'm too scared.

~ Healing Wolf ~

December – Month Twelve

PRISON LIFE

Then hope is born in the protection of the Men's Support Group, and the future opens. No longer are beggars afraid or ashamed, but willing to say "fuck-it" to the tired old ways and build and start to build anew! Now even the fights are new, the fight to reclaim one's soul.

There are moments of clarity and the irony of finding goodness, greatness, and even love in prison. Lowering our masks risks exposing our brokenness in new ways. Loving now interferes with every thought.

Taking a real good look, you think we see something new. What would be different if I gave someone a hand, or they gave me a hand? Because as monsters, we're also brothers, sons, husbands, dads, and uncles...and in-laws.

We spend years alone with our own thoughts, pretending not to feel our brokenness. Finally, tired of watching death in motion, or fellow cons getting old, "psych meds" for the walking dead in this combat zone. Demons chew on the fabric of our souls, pretending, some play too rough on the wings of evil. Finally, we peer beyond the stone walls into our mind's eye and are tempted to just end it.

Have You Ever

॰ॐ॰

Have you ever felt pain or despair?

Have you ever needed someone but no one was there?

Have you ever thought you were losing your mind?

And there just isn't any way to avoid it that you can find?

Have you ever told yourself you got to hang on?

Have you ever looked around and everyone was gone?

Had you ever had to fight to be strong?

Have you ever thought you were part of a team and been wrong?

Have you ever been locked up in the pen?

Have you ever seen what prison does to men?

~ Painted King ~

Lost in the Wind

❧

From the cradle to the grave, this life was fatal for Ray.
Stuck on the other side, heard my mother cry as she waited for me.
Is this my destiny, to be stuck in a jail cell?
Ain't nothin' left in me; I'm going through another trial
'cause my little dog left me to face this world all alone shedding tears in
misery as I call my home. How can I be blamed? Forgive me Lord:
I'm insane, in search of fame, it won't hurt to change, lost in this
whirlwind of sin; why did you follow me? Again and again? I hear you
calling me, memories of your laughter and smile as a child and after a
while I seen your "capture me" style from playing ball on a summer day
to the halls living life as a runaway. I hear the gun blaze in my sleep, and
now you rest in peace. See, what you fools don't understand is that this
game is for keeps. Now the street is a place you could be swallowed by
death; brothers taking each other's live and going to rest in peace.
In this cold world, I wanted more for you; the Lord knows for all you
fools, I want the world for you 'cause I love you, so recognize that life
goes on. See the pain in my eyes, so learn from right from wrong
and the rest of my life (because you chose to go before me)
is dedicated to you, my little Dog, my primo, my homie.
I love you, fool.

> Lost another; man I'm going crazy;
> Dear Lord can you save me, vision's getting
> hazythink about our babies, trapped in this
> life of sin. Dear Lord daily I'm getting lost
> in the wind.

~ Unknown ~

If You Haven't Done Time You Don't Know

The confinement is like pressure
inside the body and out, with unrelenting dread.

The isolation of being surrounded by 100's of hostile men
who don't care & don't want to know of my loneliness?

Disconnection from everyone who has a piece of my heart
as I desperately hold on to the pieces of their hearts I have.

Strangeness, unfamiliarity & ugliness of the homeless hearts
inside these others like me.

The huge hatreds, violence and fears hunting the cages.

Guilty days hounded by the destruction left on the outside.

Odd disconnection's with the outside that twist my heart.

The horror of fatherless children
tracing the death walk to prison.

The last good-bye to the loved one who couldn't hold on,
prisoner burn-out.

I resist saying: "Fuck-it"…then wondering why.

Looking for meaning in-between
wondering, what is it you think you know?

~ *Healing Wolf* ~

The Cost of Fun

As I sit here all alone in this twisted world of steel and stone it dawns on me that there is no one I can trust, every one is selfish and unjust.

I think back to all the years gone by, I think of all the good men who had to die. Prison is a wound that swells and festers, it's stocked with punks, rapist and sick ass chesters.

We try to forget how we make our loved ones cry. They shake their heads and ask us why? We consider our sorry ass lives only as good as our prison made knives.

We bend the rules to meet our own needs. Who cares if someone has to bleed?

If I could turn back time and do it all again, would I still commit the same sin? Sadly I can't say yes or no the truth is I just don't know.

I always had scooters, cash and a good gun, now I am doing life in prison; so was it worth the fun?

~ Painted King ~

Only What the Eyes Can See

≈

If you think you know me…
you don't.

If you believe I am only what your eyes see
you are not looking deeper in to mine.

My color, and shape
are only a reflection of blood and some borrowed DNA
of those who brought me here.

In here also lives something
more obscure and complex
than just this accused and guilty body of flesh.

It is an eternal fire…
passed down by the very beginnings of all generations.

It cannot be seen, or heard by eyes
formed out of looking only at the shelter of this light.

I am not going to explain why
I have this moment with you.

I will only say;
you are my brother.

I am not what you see
while I am speaking in my own voice…

I am what you feel in that single moment
when you finally open your eyes.

So, please hear me well,
and we will speak again.

~ Fierce Fox ~

Unknown

~

Do this one thing

just this one thing

like it's the only thing

and do it till

it opens a vein

cracks the dike

till it hurts

because it isn't real

until it hurts.

~ Shaman's Key ~

A Poem Not Open for Opinion

Please don't pretend you care.
Can't give up - I hear
"Be strong and patient..."
It all sounds so good.
Well, what do they know; let them spend a day
in my life.
See how they like to eat the food I eat
The bed I sleep on,
the lock downs, The many faceless faces - looking at empty dreams,
the false hopes, the close environment I live in.
See how they like all those eyes on them.
Where? On this piece of land
"of nothing goes un-noticed."
Oh, what about the never ending waiting for the moment
that won't arrive but, so desired.
So?
What do you think now?
How does it all sound to you?
Do you have a solution?
No?

I didn't think so;
Yes, I am a convict, an inmate maybe the worst of humanity;
what makes you so great to cast judgment
or to offer false hope?
How much time is enough?
Two-maybe Three lives.
Maybe an eternity?
Oh but don't kid yourself
I am,
but a mere human
unlike you.
I won't be around forever
So let it be it,
or let me be.

~ Fierce Fox ~

Prison Boots

~

Let me tell you about myself,
How I came to be and who I am.
I'm neither a flower, a stone, or a man.
But here in prison, sooner or later,
Together we'll stand.
I see others like me walking by.
Dark brown skin all shiny and new.
Laughing to myself, Ha!
These new guys, haven't a clue.
I've walked many a mile within walls,
Seen'em stand-seen'em fall, I've run from the cops
I've kicked them in their balls.
I've been sold, given away,
Passed around and used.
Walked on, stomped on, kicked around and abused.
Hell - it was just another day;
I was tied up and thrown in the trash.
Just to be pulled out of this,
Crazy mother fucker - on a mission to thrash.
I had no choice, I had to ride.

It's the life I've been given
I choose no sides.
No pride, do or die.
Now I'm old and smelly
My skin is cracked and peeled.
I won't last much longer, I know my fate is sealed.
But from behind these walls
I've put in my work-watched you come in from the street,
Walked with you every mile - and protected your
Nasty stinking feet.
But it was all for nothing,
Because nobody gives a hoot
About a wore out pair of
Prison Boots.

~ Indio ~

Untitled Number Five

In this pressure cooker,
The lines are hard,
And the rules are serious,
Keeping some aware.

Behind vicious whispers,
Smiling enemies plot.
Traps to be avoided,
Stalkers to watch,
Pressure unrelenting.

Warily he tracks my step,
Always aware of my presence,
Calculating my attitude,
And searching my eyes.

In truth, he's only suspicious,
Not aware of the real danger,
He's putting himself to sleep,
Cause waiting tires him out…

~ Healing Wolf ~

Lost and Found

❦

A funny thing happened to me the other day, while I was walking the prison yard. Just for a brief moment a warm feeling came over me.

The only way I can really describe it is, it's kinda like brushing up against a tree. It's there for a second and then it's gone.

It doesn't happen very often and has only happened since I've been locked up in prison, which has been ten years now.

There is something very familiar about the feeling, like its part of who I used to be. So why does it feel so strange? And why can't I put my finger on it? And why is it only with me for so short a time?

Wait a minute. There it is again, that feeling. What the hell is that sensation I keep brushing up against?

Hold on. I think I'm beginning to understand, it's something I lost many years ago and I didn't even realize I had lost it until I started looking for it.

That thing I keep brushing up against and that feeling that only touches me for a moment....is happiness.

~ *Indio* ~

Yard Birds

Seagulls, dump ducks, flying rats, rat with feathers, flying shit houses, flying garbage cans, no good filthy disgusting disease ridden birds!

Over the years I have listened to people ridicule and degrade these beautiful birds. Guards, prisoners and free people, all seem to say a lot of the same hateful things about the seagulls.

And I just don't get it! Don't feed those nasty bastards or I'll write you a 115, a guard says to me.

Don't you just hate those good for nothing filthy creatures? All they do is shit on my new car, a free man say's to me.

Well, fuck your 115! And fuck your yard jacket! And especially fuck your new car!

Doesn't anybody see the big picture anymore? Is that little bird shit hitting you on the shoulder really going to cramp your style that much? You would think that especially the men in prison would be extremely thankful for any wild life willing to show itself in this fucked up environment.

I would gladly take a hit from bird shit just to be able to enjoy the sight of birds in circled flight. Like an oil painting comes to life before my eyes, art that has been sculpted by Grandfather's hands Himself.

Do you think you're any better or cleaner than a yard bird? Have you ever really thought about how much waste one human being creates in one day?

After all, seagulls don't pollute the ocean with millions of gallons of oil a year, they're not responsible for global warming, or the production of massive nuclear weapons.

Just think about it for a moment, the same way a lot
of you views seagulls is not a whole lot different than
the way society views' prisoners, walking shit houses,
walking garbage cans, scum of the earth, no good
filthy disgusting disease ridden jail birds!
Now if you had wings, do you think you would drop
a turd on the head of people who have oppressed and
humiliated you?
You're damn right! I sure the hell would.

~ Indio ~

Encased in Stone

～

Encased in stone reinforced with steel,
faded pain covers the history on the cement walls.
As I walk the tier to the moldy shower stall with the barred door,
I notice the dark stain on the floor that at one time was
blood that flowed in a living mans veins.
Encased in stone reinforced with steel
I pace eight steps to the door
and then eight steps back to the wall,
my mind alert to any noise
that don't fit into the normal roar of my world.
Encased in stone reinforced with steel
I lay on my bunk and wonder how many guys
have laid on this thin wore out mattress
wondering how many guys have laid on it before them
or how many more will before they throw it away?
Encased in stone reinforced with steel
I rip open the paper bag that holds what
passes for today's lunch,
a paper cup with a spoonful of
hard peanut butter,
a soft apple
and four slices of bread
and this time only two of them are hard.
Encased in stone reinforced with steel,
how can I find words to tell you
how the hole feels??

~ *Painted King* ~

Liar

~

Why does anyone find it hard to say what's real? Say what you mean, to hell with how anyone may feel. If they can't deal with the truth they can't deal with what's real.

If they can't deal with the truth they are weak. This is life there is not room for the meek.

If every one told the truth life would be easy. You would know who's good and who's sleazy.

If you got to lie your doing something wrong. Face the facts it won't last that long. Sooner or later you will get busted, and life sucks when you can't be trusted.

Say how it is and how you feel. If they can't deal with that they can't deal with what's real.

Liar when you see me don't even bother to speak. Why in the hell would I want to hear any one that fucking weak?

~ Painted King ~

Nothing Left

In times of loneliness and pain
You see there is little left to gain.
When times are hard and you're left to suffer alone,
You can almost feel your heart turning to stone.
When you have seen the blood and heard the never ending scream,
You soon give up all your useless hopes and dreams.
In times of loneliness and pain
There is little left to gain,
All that's left is finding out how long it takes you to go insane.

~ *Painted King* ~

Just Monsters

Today I walked the yard;
I saw the hunger in so many eyes.
So many men not knowing where to turn
Or where to go from where they stand,
Only knowing they got to do something,
Because the place they are standing right now
Is killing them and it's killing them real slow.
The prisons in this state demand we become monsters
Or we become nothing at all.
What diversions we once had are now gone,
Nothing replaced them but emptiness.
All around me I see the lost lonely look
In the eyes of men the state has tagged monsters.
We're not monsters;
We're brothers, sons, dads, uncles, and husbands.
We're men who have been fucked over
And forced to face a life we didn't want
And didn't ask for. We only lived it the best way we knew how.
No one told us how to do it, no one gave us any leadership.
No one cared how we did it as long as we didn't cross the line.
That line that kept the haves from the has nots.
Well I crossed that fucking line.
I was one of them have nots.
I had that same hungry look in my eyes back then.
I needed more than I had so I became a monster
Or so I'm told.
And being as I have had that hungry look in my eyes
I know it when I see it
And it's all around me hid behind three dollar kid's.
If we weren't such state made monsters
We would work together and feed this hunger that's killing us,
But then we're just monsters
Or so we are told

~ Painted King ~

393

Why the Strings Don't Sing

～

They used to sing against the big gray wall
everyday, all day,
singing to the black bird to the little boy blue
with twelve steel tongues that danced along the board
and sang and sang and sang
and sang while mother died
and sang while brother died
and sang when the road was too long
when sleepless terror began to steal memories away
and sang that the love of God was not a poster of kittens
that there was no line to sign on
when redemption begins
and off the big gray wall
steel tongues sang
and sang and sang and sang
trying to make the wall come down.
And I tried to give the song to someone else
to help him break the wall
but he chose instead to sleep in wine and needles

and I wish it was different but that's the way it is
and the song became numbers, dates in a book
names on a list, a science I taught,
swallowed dignity and anger,
a sweeping of corridors and a futile belief that songs
make walls come down.
There are blackbirds and little boys blue
who have never heard the strings
singing against the big gray wall.
There are orphans asleep in wine and needles,
the illustrated fatherless
restless in dreams of hate,
young gods without a myth.
And there are poets in voiceless grief
that their strings no longer sing.

~ Shaman's Key ~

The Flower's Will to Grow

~

Stone walls bury me,
steel re-enforced cement all around me,
trying to weigh me down and crush my will to grow.
Even with the tons of rock
the state has heaped upon my head I grow.
I refuse to held down by the massive weight.
It will take much more than the state can pile on me
to kill my will to grow into the man I hope to become.
Even in the darkest times
I find ways to reach past the heavy burden of the cement walls.
I refuse to let my will be killed.
What would become of me if I was to give up?
If I gave in to the death wish of the state
what would I become?
Stone walls bury me,
steel re-enforced cement all around me
trying to weigh me down and crush my will to grow.
But like a rare flower
I grow through the little cracks on my heavy cement world.
A flower germinated in blood
fertilized by hate
and watered by a million tears from convicted men.
still the flower grows and keeps growing;
The weight of the stone walls and re-enforced cement
will never be able to crush the flower's will to grow...

~ Painted King ~

The Last Day of February 1994

❧

The way he staggered across

the prison exercise yard

he looked like a bewildered ballerina…

hands clamped tightly to his lower abdomen

in an attempt to stem the red flow

seeping through trembling fingers,

only to pirouette lifeless

into the wet green grass

before a hundred pair of eyes

that see nothing.

~ Patrick Nolan ~

California Medical Facility, Vacaville
❧

Listless, the look
in his eye. He paces
always cutting right—
he builds boxes, you see,
his bony arms writhing
as hands flutter with
benedictions; heedless
of the shank eyes
that tear into him.
He nods and smiles,
the lint in his Don King
crown bright beneath high
ceiling lights—it doesn't
matter that his clothes
are rumpled prison blues
that don't fit—he doesn't
exist in this gray concrete
plane…except for those brief
minutes and the gold of his
fantasy shrivels into a cold
knot in the pit of his stomach.
But it doesn't last long; just
long enough for his psyche meds
to kick in.

~ *Patrick Nolan* ~

A Lot Can Be Said About Poetry
(By the Shoes a Poet Wears)

Old Folsom: sitting slouched on my spring bunk,
my feet bridge the space between bed and wall;
notebook positioned on the arc of my knees;
pen poised–
I feel the heat emanating off a 40 watt bulb
dangling inches from my left cheek
by two white wires I've plugged into the wall socket
at the back of the cell.

Five tiers times eight;
a thousand plus prisoners
beneath one green copper roof;
the gun walk so close I can spit out the black painted bars
across the open abyss and hit the cop
who makes his rounds.

My cellie sleeps,
undisturbed by the oceanic roar spilling out of the cells,
off tiers;
a waterfall of voices and sounds,
a crashing cacophony against the building's
hand hewn granite walls;
radios blast for dominance,
televisions droning, toilets flushing.

Through shattered windows
winter winds force prisoners
to burrow deep within woolen
military - like blankets stamped
"California Department of Corrections."

~ Patrick Nolan ~

What Happens When the Reason Stops

He pulls back from the square
silver - backed safety glass
cement - glued to the wall,
and allows for some light to filter in
around him emanating off the fluorescent
ceiling fixture outside the cell's locked steel door.

His face, distorted by the dark shadow play
partially reveals the left
side of his cheek.

It was the eye he recognized,
deep set, full of questions.
It could be the eye of anyone doing time who,
night after night
wakes to petition the darkness
for one more reason
not to open a vein,
and night after night
finds a reason not to.

~ Patrick Nolan ~

A Psychology on the Surrounding Environment Prison

❧

Each wall is gray;
unpainted – some with floor wax,
are polished to a high glossy sheen
almost marble in texture–
sound contained.

Green – painted steel doors with plexiglass
windows cut into them,
open and close,
electronically controlled by a cop
"correctional officer"
in a fish bowl tower
across the way
from where cells are lined two tiers high;
compartmentalized;
sealed tight against the world.

Twenty-two hours a day,
men ferment like rotting grapes,
waiting for nothing.

~ *Patrick Nolan* ~

Old Man Motown

Old Man Motown dances toe to toe
around the prison exercise track
throwing jabs as he bobs and weaves,
dressed in cutoff denim shorts
and hard - soled boots,
while young cons lay like rock lizards
bemoaning the three digit heat.

Old Man Motown
alone with his thoughts,
shoots short combinations,
counters blow for blow with some imaginary foe,
his five-foot-five frame
now heavy with age,
pushing forward against the concrete upgrade
that emanates a wall of rippling heat.

Old Man Motown
his raven wing skin
streaked white with dried sweat,
knees pulsing pistons of determination—
to see him,
this silver haired grandpa with blue cataract eye,
one can't help but smile as he dances his dance
in the sweltering northern California sun.

Old Man Motown
times have changed.
The once noble beasts
of this barren gray Savannah
are now almost extinct,
ravaged by the vicious sweep of rat packs
that make prey of the aged
sick and weak.

~ *Patrick Nolan* ~

The Ballad of Ronnie Libertine
(One Man's Luck Is Another Man's Misery)

❧

I

To the population of prisoners
that knew him, he was a crazed
caricature of what was once man;
time like an insidious worm had
gnawed away all that was sane, of Ronnie Libertine.

II

It's true, you know, prison can
change a man from bad to worse
depending on what demons chew
the fine fabric of the soul – as
for Ronnie, though having never really known him, who knows…

III

Rumors, snide remarks, laughter,
reverberate the previous day's
shooting incident of crazed Ronnie Libertine:

In broad day, wearing red
work vest, Ronnie calmly
climbed through the razor
wire fence in the prison's
inner compound, followed
quickly by five chambered rounds.

IV

It was an attempted escape
of the kind not printed
in today's newspapers…
"He was lucky he didn't die."

~ *Patrick Nolan* ~

Christmas Night

~

Scribble, scribble, scratch and write, dark little words on a Hollowed
Christmas Night.
As I lay here in the dark I can just barely see,
The black little pen and the white page that lies before me.
I was bathed in Holy Water today by the good Ole' preacher man
baptized,
drowned in the waters of Bethlehem.
Purified, reborn, forgiven for all my sins, I pray that it makes a difference
in the end.
When it's time to begin. My walk after death.
But as I lay here in the darkness of my cell,
I look up at Dream Catchers and Medicine Wheels that hang from the
ceiling.
As feathers sway and swing–swing and sway casting shadows that carry
faces,
of ghosts I cannot recognize.
Through the darkness as I'm laying on my bunk, I stare up at the metal
sheet above me,
where my celly is fast asleep, maybe.
And I can't help but wonder if he dreams the same dreams that I do?
And if I look real close could I see them flying?
And do our dreams collide within the willow hoops? Fighting one
against the other?
Or do they recognize the essence of our humanity, and help one to find
the other,
to ease our troubled minds, the bondage that cripples us.
And so I look down at the stone floor that I waxed 'over '& 'over' &
'over'
fifteen times or more, due to the compulsive disorder I've developed,
from so many years – so many tears, behind this door.
Every little hair, crumb or speck of dirt, weighs heavy upon my
shoulders.

Even now in this darkness, I feel like cleaning it.
And the shirts tied to the line at the end of my bed, seem to stand at
attention in single file,
like ghostly medieval soldiers, protecting the dead.
And this flat, black-faced TV, stares back at me in the night,
No pictures–no sound, mocking me.
That is where I learned of new inventions, the changing times,
new Presidents, new wars, the things that are going on in the real world.
The Outside World. I have had so many fantasies, companion
adventures,
and love affairs within this Black Box, Newscasters & TV Stars,
Judge Judy & Janet Reno, I've sipped wine and made love to them all.
A disturbing, pathetic life for a man, to look for the company of a
woman,
within a box–while living in a box.
But now it's cold, flat blank expression seems to laugh at me,
as if to enjoy the loneliness that haunts me
As I lay here in the dark on this "Hallowed Christmas Night,"
I can almost see tall black trees swaying within the forest of my cell –
The Jungle of my mind.
As flat black snakes slither across the reflection of this over waxed floor.
And old Indians & little green Leprechauns and angels bathed in white.
All seem to be singing a haunting melody
On this cold, dark "Christmas Night."

~ Indio ~

405

Convicts Christmas

❧

A pissed off convict with a sneer on his face,
my bros are out partying and the pigs got me locked up
in this rat ass place.
It's gonna be a fucked up year
I see this already,
the chow sucks and the never ending chatter is loud and steady.
It looks like no harleys or pussy again this year,
damn how many is it I spent in here?
Yeah, it's Christmas but who even gives a fuck?
They're just gonna feed us some processed turkey
that tastes like a hockey puck.
Hurry up fuckers move your asses.
Well now ain't this just the story of my life?
Some lucky ass rookie just found my knife.
Looks like I'll spend Christmas in the hole,
washing my boxers in the toilet bowl.
It's not good then it's not that damn bad
and it sure as hell won't be the worst Christmas
this convict ever had…

~ Painted King ~

Rebecca

☞

Rebecca, insane at last
as we all knew she would be
the veil finally stripped away by brutal love
more brutal than the love she got
at the hand of a shrieking mother
who kicked her in the stomach
called he "whore" at the age of ten
after her brother had raped her.

Rebecca, insane at last
those dark wounded eyes
in the round soft face of a child of twenty six
scratching at my window at three in the morning
wet with rain, forcing me to see what I had done to her
when I withdrew love.
It was now when I treated her the worst
she desired me the most and made sacrifices.

. Rebecca, insane at last a cold white hand
floating in a tub of milky red water and Jean Nate'
Shoulder and head leaning to one side:
The death of Marat; damp black hair stuck to tiles
once held to a lover's face like a bouquet of roses
blue lips vaguely smiling as she punished us.

~ *Shaman's Key* ~

Good Byes

~

I've said good-byes

and missed a few

and I've got to say

I would trade all

the good-byes

for the ones I missed.

~ Shaman's Key ~

A Hard Way To Go

~

I live behind hard walls that hold hard rules
that govern hard men.

Any goodness that slips out of me unexpectedly
is usually greeted hard heartedly.

Between me & my healthy self are hard lines.

Crossing those lines usually ends up in hard feelings.

So, when I come to Circle to make hard choices

I really don't want to end up in a hard place.

So, show me compassionately to get past my hard heartedness,
to where I don't have to be hard to be safe!

~ Healing Wolf ~

On Earth

∿

On Earth there's a convict
with & without parole,
an artist, and poet!
On Earth there's a clown
livin' it's own world,
and in a world of illusions
that you will never know,
nor understand
unless you fully get to know
the worth within this convict
carries alone.

~ Significant Elk Who Soars ~

The Folsom State Prison Experience

It was a quiet calm Monday afternoon inside Folsom Prison walls. I felt unease with the peacefulness around me, knowing that this is a level four prison and violence could occur at any moment, but I pushed the negative thoughts aside and continued on discussing strategy for our next soccer game.

Our peacefulness was broken with the sound of an alarm; within seconds the loud speaker on the yard announced. "yard down!' Everybody rushed to find a decent spot to sit down. After four years in prison, I still get startled hearing the threatening announcement, "Yard down!"

As I sat there, sad and worried thoughts rushed through my mind; I wondered is this false alarm, or did someone really get hurt. I sat in a dazed wonder and watched all the correctional officers in a confused state running to the place of the alarm.

This time someone did get hurt. A stretcher rushed by with an inmate laying on his stomach motionless, blood flowing from his neck and from the side of his stomach. Medical personnel tried to stop the blood, but it didn't work.

Did something he do warrant such a punishment? I sat there in disbelief, thinking: Did he have a chance to explain himself before he was attacked? My confused mind kept questioning, "Did he know it was coming and did he have a chance to talk to his loved ones before this happened?" I know his mom is crying over his suffering – just like mine would.

Why can't we look at another human being and see that, that person is also in the same pain and sadness just like everyone else? Why do we have to show how tough and macho we are by hurting someone else? I am sick and tired of all this macho tough image crap.

I wonder is he going to make it? All these questions I have will never be answered, because I am afraid to know. "Note:" I found out later that he did survive the attack.

~ Unknown ~

Authors Index

413

419

Acknowledgments

This book could not have been written without the assistance of the inmates of Folsom State Prison, inmates of New Folsom Prison, and many other people. Any omissions are accidental and due to a faulty memory:

Patrick Nolan

Scott Nolan

Margaret Ryan

Jim Carlson

Dennis Merino

John Javna

Bill Wich

Lynn Canney

Eldra Jackson III

Rick Misener

Martin Williams

Aaron Patrick Ramey

Manuel Ruiz

Rob Allbee

Scott Kernan

Aaron Ortega

Lonnie Jackson

Stefano Landini

David Loofbourrow

Paul Brar

Margaret Dominguez

Doug Sooley

Michael Conyers

Itamar Vinitzky

Roland Stoecker

Michael Peatrowsky

Michael Owens

Ken T. Allen

Tuan Doan

Gonzalo Alvarado

Kosal Khiev

James Street

James McLeary

Gethin Aldous

Steven Spitzer

Bharataji Joplin

Brad Bunnin

Victor Green

David Holland

Lyle Nooner

Martin Marks

CPSIA information can be obtained
at www.ICGtesting.com
Printed in the USA
BVHW050859231121
622343BV00004B/59